Praise for *Executive Presence*

"*Executive Presence* shows us that there is an art to communication and a recipe for successful personal branding. Harrison shares this with us step by step, all the while honing our social intelligence and raising our social IQ."
—Roy S. Ritenour, Vice President, Hertz Corporation

"It's critically important for senior executives—people from all ranks, really—to be inclusive in their communication, to show empathy and listen to colleagues and peers with intent. Harrison's thinking on social intelligence and his ability to provide executives with a step-by-step guide to succeed in interpersonal relations on the corporate battlefield is a testament to his own mastery of the topic. *Executive Presence* is a must-have for the modern executive's reading list."
—Brian Murphy, Ph.D., Chairman and CEO, PrimeStar Solar Inc.

"Effective presence is as elusive as fine art. Harrison Monarth has captured it in *Executive Presence.*"
—David Watterson, Jr., Ph.D., Executive and Leadership Consultant, Watterson and Associates

"If you want a powerful executive presence, then you need a strong personal brand. In this compelling book, Harrison proves that controlling how you're perceived is the path to having a successful career. With practical advice and real-life examples, you'll learn how to stand out, get attention, and protect yourself. Read this book before your competition does!"
—Dan Schawbel, bestselling author of *Me 2.0* and award-winning blogger at PersonalBrandingBlog.com

"It is not enough, by far, to be good or even great at what you do anymore. To truly get noticed and ascend to leadership in business and the corporate environment, a unique mix of self-promotion, social skills, and empathy is required to get to the top spot. Harrison Monarth delivers the tools to get you there in his new book *Executive Presence.* This dynamic book can help anyone who wants to become more successful in their profession."
—Debbie Allen, bestselling author of *Confessions of Shameless Self Promoters*

"*Executive Presence* is the first major work to utilize a genuinely rhetorical approach to the study of persuasion. So much is written about what *should* be persuasive; this work properly focuses on what *will* be persuasive. Harrison Monarth is one of the very few writers to recognize that all persuasion originates in the persuader's choices and that "spin" is involved in *all* persuasion, not just *misleading* persuasion. He also recognizes the crucial element of persuader's choices as to what is the topic and the meaning argued for as well as its ethical implications.
—Richard E. Vatz, Ph.D., Towson Distinguished Professor, Professor, MCOM/COMM; University Senate; Towson University, Thomas Szasz Civil Liberties Award, Associate Psychology Editor, *USA Today* magazine; Editor, *Current Psychology*

"Harrison has been a valuable contributor to our magazine, shining an illuminating light onto the world of learning and development for our readers. This book promises to be as entertaining, relevant, well written, and—most importantly—as instructive as his column, and I'll be studying the communication and influencing techniques he outlines in it closely."
—Elizabeth Eyre, Content Publisher, *Training Journal*

Executive Presence

Executive Presence

The Art of Commanding Respect
Like a CEO

Harrison Monarth

To Andy —
Great working with you!

All the Best,
H.

Mc Graw Hill

New York   Chicago   San Francisco   Lisbon   London
Madrid   Mexico City   Milan   New Delhi   San Juan
Seoul   Singapore   Sydney   Toronto

5 6 7 8 9 0 DOC/DOC 1 5 4 3 2

ISBN: 978–0–07–163287–4
MHID: 0–07–163287–5

This publication is designed to provide accurate and authoritative information in regard to the subject matter covered. It is sold with the understanding that the publisher is not engaged in rendering legal, accounting, or other professional service. If legal advice or other expert assistance is required, the services of a competent professional person should be sought.
> —*From a Declaration of Principles Jointly Adopted by a Committee of the American Bar Association and a Committee of Publishers and Associations*

McGraw-Hill books are available at special quantity discounts to use as premiums and sales promotions, or for use in corporate training programs. To contact a representative please visit the Contact Us pages at www.mhprofessional.com.

This book is printed on acid-free paper.

Library of Congress Cataloging-in-Publication Data
Monarth, Harrison.
    Executive presence : the art of commanding respect like a CEO / by Harrison Monarth.
        p. cm.
    ISBN 0–07–163287–5 (alk. paper)
1. Executive ability. 2. Communication in management. 3. Interpersonal communication. 4. Interpersonal relations. I. Title.
    HD38.2.M647 2010
    658.4'092—dc22   2009016400

To Asli

Contents

Part III: A Brand Is a Promise: What Does Your Personal Brand Say?

Part IV: The Age of 24-Hour Media: If You're Not On, You're Out

Part V: Reputation Management: Your Good Name Is All You Have

Foreword

HARRISON MONARTH'S *Executive Presence* is essential reading for anyone desiring to rise up out of obscurity in our corporate existence. From the moment we step into our offices, and all the day long until sleep mercifully shuts our cares away, we are immersed in combat. Either we will wreak our will—prevail—or we will fail. Mr. Monarth writes with clarity and zest. He is in full command of his materials. Not only does he never permit psychosociological claptrap to clutter his prose; he transcends it, keeping his thinking bright and clear. Among his several major theses—all useful—is his paramount contention about "social intelligence." Our relations with subordinates, peers, and superiors in the corporate battleground are critically a matter of perception—our own, about the impact that our arguments per se may be having on other people, but also of the instant judgments that are being formed about us on an irrelevant personal basis. Sun Tzu could not have put the terms of engagement more subtly. We must understand our vulnerability. We are neither superior to the impact of our personalities nor independent of how they may be perceived. The battle is won or lost not so much because of the cogency of our position but often because of the chords that our manner of speaking, dress, deportment, or attitude strike on the sympathies of others. Social intelligence is the critical factor in any contest of wills. I am grateful to Mr. Monarth for his wisdom."

—Reid Buckley, President of The Buckley School of
Thought, Reflection, and Communications

Acknowledgments

My FIRST ACKNOWLEDGMENT has to go to my wonderful literary agent, Rita Rosenkranz, who persistently checked in on me to see how my proposal was coming along once I mentioned I had an idea for another book. Without her, this would still be a half-baked idea languishing in a paper pile on the landfill that is my desk. I can't say enough about her thoughtful guidance and unmatched expertise in preparation of this project. I'm also forever grateful to my champion at McGraw-Hill, senior editor Donya Dickerson, one of the nicest people you could meet, in- or outside of the publishing world, whose enthusiastic support and expert coaching along the way of creating this work made this a better book.

I salute my colleagues who've contributed their wisdom and ideas to this book.   Prof. Richard E. Vatz of Towson University is one of them. His work and writing has inspired me from the day I became aware of it. His brilliance certainly influenced the way I think and write about persuasive communication. There are many others to which I owe thanks—who've become my teachers and mentors, sometimes unbeknownst to them. Among them, Hy Bender, whose input during the proposal stage was crucial. Larry Brooks, a good friend and brillant editor, inspired my writing. Also, Reid Buckley, the brilliant curmudgeon and fellow speech coach whose work energizes me when I'm at a loss for words. I owe a great debt to my many clients who've made it possible for me to become an expert in the field I love—and who've afforded me the luxury of becoming a writer.

My good friends deserve an enormous amount of credit for keeping me sane and productive during the writing of this book. Paul Isherwood whose friendship and stimulating conversation make our coffeehouse visits and workouts at the gym a time I treasure and regularly look forward to. And Mehmet Kazgan graciously makes sure that I don't have to battle technology problems, as I type away through the night at my computer. You're a life-saver. A special thank you goes to Sue Blake, my dear friend and the best publicist an author could wish for. Sue is directly and indirectly responsible for most of the great press I get. The friendship that developed from our association is something I cherish. My sweet Mom, Roswitha, is alive and well in my heart. And finally, love to my father, who's always happy to hear from me and whose pride in me is palpable.

To them and the usual suspects—you know who you are—I owe my joie de vivre.

Executive Presence

Introduction

IN HIS HIT television series *Celebrity Apprentice*, Donald Trump made this jarring remark: "There are winners and losers. And most people are losers." On a human level, that's clearly wrong. I'd argue that every breath even the humblest soul takes is a triumph and that everyone whom that person loves and who loves him or her in return represents a monumental victory.

In terms of careers, however, Trump's statement contains a kernel of truth, and that is why he received zero flack for making it. Trump was saying out loud what millions of business leaders really think. It's not that most people lack intelligence or skill or even ambition, but they haven't learned how to leverage their assets by effectively representing themselves or communicating with others to the best of their abilities.

For example, chances are that you have at least a few friends and colleagues who have enormous talent but somehow never achieve the success their level of work deserves. At the same time, you probably can think of a number of people who don't appear to have much going for them yet do extremely well. The typical buzz about such people is that "she's good at office politics" or "he's connected." That's echoed in one of the most common phrases uttered about business: "It's not what you know; it's who you know." As with the Trump pronouncement, this cliché isn't quite on target, but if we adjust it to "It's not only what you know but how you manage perception," we are taking the first steps on a life-altering journey.

Although it may seem unfair, the reality is that being skilled at one's chosen profession isn't enough. Toiling away in obscurity and hoping the world will notice has never been a sound strategy, and neither is managing to grab attention but then failing to show off one's greatest strengths.

Think of it this way: The male lion isn't the smartest animal in the jungle; great apes, elephants, and parrots are all more intelligent. Nor is he the largest animal or, for that matter, the largest cat (the tiger is). He isn't even the best hunter among his own pride; it's his female mate that tracks and subdues prey. Why is the male lion considered the king of the jungle? Because he has an impressive mane and an even more impressive roar.

This doesn't mean the lion is a fraud: If called upon, he can back up that roar in spades. However, what makes the lion special is the combination of his genuine power with an image and related behavior that effectively communicates that power to the world.

If you want to be a lion—that is, the king or queen of your chosen profession—you need to adopt the same approach. The good news is that you don't have to be born with great looks, or a silver spoon in your mouth, or any other unique asset. You can start out with no money, no friends, and no connections. All you need is the will to succeed and the state-of-the-art techniques provided in the book you are holding.

What I'm offering isn't mere theory but the results of extensive trial-and-error experience, the latest scientific research in interpersonal communication and human behavior, and intensive one-on-one coaching with top-level executives and professionals.

I'm the founder and president of GuruMaker, an internationally respected consulting firm that helps Fortune 500 executives, international politicians, and other high-profile professionals sharpen their communication, persuasion, perception management, and media skills. The strategies this book describes have been developed over decades and field-tested by thousands of clients. A modern professional needs to master a multitude of communication skills to create an *executive presence* and reach the top in his or her field. These skills range from accurately reading people and predicting their behavior to subtly influencing the perceptions and behavior of those around you, from persuading those of opposing views to come over to your side to creating and maintaining a personal brand that broadcasts your positive reputation to a wide audience, and from managing and controlling your online reputation to performing effective damage control when things go wrong. If you've ever wondered how to conduct a difficult conversation you needed to have, how to best resolve the conflicts that arise in any interpersonal business relationship, or how to negotiate crisis situations that threaten to harm your good reputation, this book will provide the answers.

The competition is tough, and intelligence and good social skills are only a ticket for admission to a successful career and business. By studying and mastering the ideas and strategies I've laid out in *Executive Presence: The Art of Commanding Respect Like a CEO*, you will gain an important edge in your quest to become a winner in your chosen field.

PART I

IMPRESSION MANAGEMENT AND THE PERCEPTIONS OF THE PUBLIC

The Natural Laws of Perception: How the People around You Perceive You

WE ARE AT our core a society of pitchers. No, we're not talking baseball here, though we all certainly wind up and deliver—and, on a regular basis, square off against—the occasional metaphoric curveball, brush-back, and unfairly called third strike. Pitching—the kind that pleads a case and asks for the order, that wraps an agenda within a message and ties a neat bow of sincerity around it—is the very essence of commerce, the lifeblood of law and politics and romance (closely aligned endeavors that they are), the fundamental stuff of human interaction.

We pitch our beliefs and our dreams to our children. We pitch our qualifications at job interviews. We plead our case in courtrooms and at bars over drinks. We manage employees by pitching them our wisdom and our vision for the future. Our leaders pitch to us every election year with more sliders and screwballs and split-fingered high heat than any reasonable spring training can or should accommodate. We are pitching when we sell, when we lobby, when we complain, and when we seek to be heard and understood, which for most of us happens each and every day.

That particular common denominator—being *understood*—is where the asterisk appears among the universe of people communicating with one another. All pitches, and more aptly all pitchers, are not created equal, and the most persuasive among us, those who continually close the deal and get the nod and generally seem to skate through life without a fallen tree on the road, much less an audit, know something the rest of us don't. They know that the art and craft of communicating do not arise from the same base level of human instinct as do walking and laughing and that taking it for granted or, worse, failing to understand and factor in the dynamics of successful communication is a recipe for randomness and mediocrity. This is precisely where the old adage "you win some and you lose some" comes from. Somebody doesn't get it because somebody *else* does.

In short, consistently successful communicators—whether sales professionals, politicians, lawyers, managers, parents, partners, or coaches—know how to manage and influence the way they are *perceived*. More than that, they understand that it is perception, not intention or even content, that dictates the outcome of an agenda that resides at the heart of each and every pitch we make. We don't—or shouldn't—talk to hear ourselves speak; we always have information to convey, a point to make, an opinion to sway, a decision to influence, an outcome we seek to manifest. Even if we are simply commiserating or analyzing, there is an agenda in play, at the heart of which is the desire to be *understood* and be taken seriously by those who can help us along our career path.

In essence, we are always pitching and have been since our first cries for food or attention were shrieked from the crib. For those who wish to improve their pitching proficiency by learning to control the way they are perceived, certain principles and natural laws make the learning curve both accessible and intuitively easy to ascend.

The Path to Perception

The way we are perceived by those who experience what we say or do or even our mere presence is the product of a specific neurological process whose outcome can take any number of forms. Information is taken in by one or more of five sensory portals—the senses—and then is filtered or processed by a suite of specific mental mechanisms that assign meaning and nuance to what has arrived through the senses, each with very different criteria and experiential rationales. From there, the information in its new, processed form—in other words, the way it is perceived—is deleted, distorted, or generalized, leading to a response that is manifested as an outcome.

That response, science tells us, has as much to do with the emotional *state* prompted by the *way* information is processed as it does with the content of the information. You may not think you like a certain type of food, but if smelling it unexpectedly makes you hungry—a direct contradiction to your experiential basis and learned bias— you may decide to take a risk and go for it. The same thing goes for accepting a meeting or placing your vote or adopting a philosophy. All bets are off because the line between input and output is anything but straight and is not remotely simple. This is the source of our opportunity as communicators, because if we know what we're doing, we can be the architects of that line.

Clearly, perception involves a lot more than listening. There are five means of input, followed by five means of filtering or processing the incoming information, leading to three possible outcomes, each of them the result of a bottom-line perception. Although deletion and distortion are rarely desired outcomes, generalization isn't necessarily bad, especially if you've positioned your message to be perceived to be correct, good, attractive, and valuable. However, nothing is certain in the sensory process, and one person's silk purse can, however inconceivably, be transformed into another's sow's ear as it navigates the harrowing process of filtering in the mind of the observer. For example, someone with a long-standing penchant for ethnic food—an experiential filter—may respond favorably to a recommendation for a new Mexican restaurant in town, whereas someone else with a different experiential filter hearing the same recommendation, even though he or she also enjoys ethnic food, may send out for Chinese instead. "To each his own" has never been truer than it is when it refers to the way people filter information.

However, good outcome or bad, you can't get to the result you want without passing through the often rusty gate of human perception with all its pitfalls. The good news is that if you do it right, you'll find inherent opportunities. Because no two people bring the same set of criteria—tastes, biases, experiences, and preferences—to the process of filtering information, identical sets of information can have very different outcomes among different recipients; that is why some people like country music and others prefer jazz. The more you know about your target audience, the more you can apply your working knowledge of the perception process to the generation of a favorable outcome.

How Messages and Signals Enter Our Awareness

It isn't enough to write off the way people take in information as a function of the five senses, because what doesn't look good or sound good on the surface may lead to an unexpected outcome after that information has been filtered. It is important to understand how all the senses can, to some extent, become arrows in the quiver of an enlightened communicator. Let's face it, unless we're serving appetizers while we make a pitch, taste isn't the first sense that comes into play.

Every day thousands of people are pulled over for speeding. Nearly every one of them says the same thing, some version of "Gee, I wasn't aware I was going too fast" or "I'm so sorry, but I'm late for [insert an empathy-eliciting excuse here]." The evidentiary facts are always the same—they were driving over the speed limit and they have something to say in their defense—and that raises the question of how some of them get off with a warning and others drive away with a ticket. Same laws, same violation, different outcomes. The explanation resides in what is *not* the same: different law enforcement officers who bring different biases and experiences (not the least of which is their mood at the moment), different pitches delivered with varying levels of skill, and a vast matrix of different tones, visual modes, and smells (think alcohol, perfume, body odor, etc.).

Chances are that someone dressed nicely with a humble countenance driving a nice car—not too nice, though, because a Ferrari might threaten the ego bias of the working-class officer—who doesn't reek of martinis and makes a sensible pitch, with a little luck thrown in (luck in this case being the mood of the officer, over which the pitcher has no control), has a better chance of a good outcome than does someone with an equally sensible pitch driving a 1980s dented car painted with gang signs with expired plates while wearing a death metal graphic T-shirt and listening to a Snoop Dog CD with the scent of illegal herbs wafting from the window. These are blatantly obvious triggers of perception, but you get the point: The pitch itself is almost totally dependent on the vehicle (in this case literally) of delivery. Before you leap to generalize these cues, you should realize that for some officers they may be the very things that elicit their empathy and prompt them to let the driver off with a warning. Yes, Snoop Dog has legions of fans, and some of them are cops.

Regardless of which mode of entry the target uses to gather information from the communicator—visual, auditory, kinesthetic (touch or pressure), smell, or taste—it all proceeds to the next step in the same fashion: It gets *filtered*. However, the mode of entry is indeed a factor in the outcome because it triggers the filtering process in ways that influence the outcome. The more personal the communication is, the more this is true. Touch and scent are big players in an exchange between lovers, friends, family members, and massage therapists, whereas they are barely on the map in a business meeting (other than a firm handshake and a compassionate touch to the elbow), town hall gathering, or presidential debate, where visual and nonverbal cues meld with auditory input to brand the message as credible or otherwise, depending on the bias of the listener.

The world watched John McCain and Barack Obama square off on television in the presidential debates, and what people saw swayed many votes. Regardless of the content of their words, both men often added value (and in some cases created a negative bias) by virtue of *how* they said what they said: everything from the looks on their faces, to the rolling of their eyes, to the timing of an impatient grin-and-bear-it contrived smile. Obama was generally cool under fire, and McCain obviously was steaming below the surface. In the first debate McCain refused to make eye contact with his opponent, and that spoke volumes to many viewers. McCain's continued reference to viewers as his "friends" triggered millions of subconscious bias programs globally, not to mention the punch lines of late-night television hosts. Minds were changed and votes were won on both sides as much for the content of their *style* as for the words they delivered, because human beings have been known to evaluate character more on the basis of style than on that of content.

It is interesting to note the change in McCain's verbal style and non-verbal cues in the second and third debates, primarily in the context of the reasons discussed here: Someone sat him down and schooled him in the wisdom of managing the perceptions he was eliciting in his audience with his impatient, intolerant tough-guy countenance. Rising executives and other professionals can learn to avoid similar initial misperceptions by reflecting on the notion that most people want to work with or for some-one—that person's competence and intelligence being a given—with social acuity and a generally pleasant disposition toward others, matters of disagreement notwithstanding. Although first impressions aren't necessar-ily written in stone, changing an established bias— this is critically impor-tant for all communicators to understand—is orders of magnitude more difficult than winning approval from an objective, nonbiased audience. In this case the bias included the party affiliation of the candidates, and for this reason among others, Barack Obama proved triumphant. The elec-tion was won on perception as much as anything else—both personal and party—and all of it entered our collective mind through the senses. That was when the filtering began.

What You're Up Against: Filters, Lenses, and Other Influencers That Distort Your Message

We have complete control over what audience members take in through their five senses. We dress ourselves, we choose what to say and how to say it, and we have entire cosmetics counters full of scents from which to choose; the mode and method of our touch are up to us, and as far as taste goes, use your imagination. The way each of those choices and their combination is perceived, however, is something over which we have absolutely no control, because that perception resides in the mind—the processing function—of the beholder, which in this case is the audience. A custom-tailored designer suit may work well in the boardroom, but it won't serve you during an interview for a programmer position at Google. The best we can do is try to understand the various filters into which sensory input flows and then optimize our choices on the basis of what we know and perceive about the target audience.

Five separate categories of filtering take place when sensory information arrives. All five connect to the five senses; for example, one's memories are applied equally to any and all of the five sensory inputs. From the field of neuro-linguistic programming (NLP) we learn that they are *meta programs, belief systems, values, memories,* and *past decisions.* Any one of these can derail your agenda, and not always for reasons you can comprehend or that make sense to you. Take the filter of *memory,* for example. All you have to do is bear a striking resemblance to someone's abusive former manager, and just about anything you say stands a good chance of deletion before you get out of the proverbial batter's box.

Meta programs involve the way people think as well as the way they approach how they think. Analogously to a computer, think of a meta program as the operating system of a person's brain, software that controls the applications that do all the real processing of incoming data. This means that the other filters—beliefs, values, memories, and past decisions—are all applications that are controlled by the operating system: the meta programs. Some people are deep thinkers; others quickly respond to surface appearances. Some people procrastinate; others go all-in quickly. Some value substance over style; others value style over substance.

The line between a meta program and a belief system can be murky: Is racial prejudice a meta program or a belief system? Both exert influence over incoming sensory input, leading to a bottom-line perception. The fact is that it doesn't matter whether it's a meta program or a belief system. What does matter is that you, as the communicator, bring a sense of how a person thinks and reacts—that person's meta programs—to the planning and execution of your pitch, your message. There are no good or bad meta programs per se; they are only the triggers that influence ensuing thought, which may or may not overturn a meta program's initial context. A meta program is not perception; it is nothing more or less than the way a person handles information, a definition of how perception will occur.

Belief systems are a can of worms. They represent a view of the world, what a person holds as true and unquestionable. Management and union leaders often clash over disparate belief systems, and the same thing can apply to environmental activists and manufacturing executives. Belief systems include deeply rooted programming that define one's worldview; they set the parameters of right and wrong and write one's personal textbook on preferences.

Belief systems include religion, cultural norms (and, for lack of a better term, *abnorms*), prejudice, educational experiences, biases, and hardwired preferences and usually stem from some combination of childhood mentoring and personal experience. They are the product of a lifetime of emotional and intellectual evolution, not always in what the masses consider the right direction. Belief systems give answers and fill the holes in what otherwise might be considered debatable or at least not provable, and because of that you and your agenda stand little chance of toppling a lifelong cherished belief. It is better to factor a belief system into your pitch and work around whatever stands ready to behead your objectives. The more you know about what enables people to make their decisions, as well as what stops them from making decisions they'd otherwise consider, the more effective you will be in crafting communications strategies that stand a chance of working.

Closely aligned with belief systems is the filter of personal *values*. Values grade things as good or bad, worthy or unworthy, appropriate or inappropriate, and dictate a memo defining how one should feel about the sensory input being processed. This feeling creates a perception, and from that perception an emotional state is manifested that leads to the ultimate disposition of the information. Anger and disgust get you deleted; excitement gets you the deal.

If what you are communicating is in conflict with the values of the receiver of the information, an immediate emotional state (sometimes thinly disguised as an opinion) that leads to a perception is created, one that says you are wrong. However, our meta programs can excuse us from following our values. Think of the senior executive who promotes a fellow Harvard alumnus instead of the more qualified candidate—an MIT graduate—vying for the same position because although he values intelligence and experience in the team, he feels no harm will come of it if once in a while he makes a different decision. Values create the *context* of a pitch, from which the receiver filters and processes all the sensory input that accompanies the pitch. Although beliefs are almost always the eliciting agent of a state, values can be circumvented more easily when the payoff is alluring enough through the creation of an emotional state that is more powerful than the value. Perhaps the most vivid example of this dynamic involves stranded survivors of disasters such as the Uruguayan rugby players who survived a plane crash in the Andes and then decided to eat the flesh of their deceased friends to remain alive. The beliefs and values remained intact but were trumped by a more powerful emotional state.

Where do belief systems and personal values come from? Certainly one source is the contextual learning and experience of the past, which aligns them closely to the next filter in the process—one's *memories*. Let's say that someone considers putting her personal values on the shelf because the potential payoff is so alluring. If, however, the last time she went this route she was so guilt-ridden that she couldn't enjoy the payoff, or perhaps things went south for her in an expected way, that memory becomes a player in the further processing of the information, tugging at the options within the filter of values until she snaps. When many of the world's financial markets virtually collapsed in late 2008, investors and the public at large heard widespread accounts of bad decision making and unethical behavior by the big banks and other financial institutions. Rising executives in the financial world, particularly those entrusted with large amounts of investors' funds, probably will experience intense scrutiny and suspicion for some time to come by a nervous public. This is the filter of memory at work, trumping the other filters, which may or may not align with that fiscal approach. As effective communicators we usually aren't privy to the memories of our audiences, and that leaves us few strategies for influencing that filter directly.

Finally, there is the filter of *past decision making*. Although it's clear that our beliefs and values often arise from our past, it is clearer that their experiential gravitas is usually the result of decisions we have made, all of which had outcomes with varying degrees of reward and pain. Nothing says learning quite like reward and pain. Hence, people's track record of decision making becomes a powerful filter of new information, sometimes independent of any beliefs or values associated with the impending perception.

Each bit of sensory input travels through this matrix of filters, influencing and shading the next, depending on one's experiences and the inherent conflict with embedded values, beliefs, and memories. All of it leads to perception, with the result being one of three things: deletion, distortion, or generalization.

Deletion, Distortion, and Generalization

Imagine someone hearing a speech from a business leader that appeals to his most dearly held social and intellectual sensibilities. The speaker looked good, delivered the speech with a pleasant tone and compelling body language, and even seemed to have what is valued in consulting circles as "beer-buddy likability." In other words, the speaker is the kind of person you'd have over for a barbeque. Then, a few minutes into the speech, the listener learns that the speaker is, of all things, a CEO whose company has a questionable environmental record. The trouble is, at least in this example, that the listener is a staunch environmental activist. For this fellow, this is the end of the filtering. It's over. The rest of the speech might as well be delivered in sign language because the information relative to the business leader's agenda has—at least as far as the environmentalist is concerned—little value. Why? Because the perceived environmental polluter has been dismissed, or *deleted*. The value and belief systems of the listener filter the incoming audio, even with its pleasant visual accessories, and render a perception. That perception becomes the listener's reality, creating an emotional state that leads to *deletion*.

That's how it works in the filtering game, and the only rules are those of the listener's creation. Logic and fairness have nothing to do with perception; they matter only in terms of the listener's *take* on logic and fairness. Sometimes information can be *partially* deleted, literally keeping what results in a positive emotional state and trashing whatever doesn't line up with the filtering beliefs, values, and memories. Of course, all this is driven by the filter of one's meta program, in which the propensity to adhere to one's values and beliefs—or not; think Eliot Spitzer—is managed and implemented.

The same thing is true of *distortion*. When we make a shift in our experience of sensory input, we are in effect making a *mis*representation of reality. In essence we are creating our own reality, one that better fits our belief system and values. In the example above, if the listener decides that the benefit to the community in the business magnate's message outweighs the drawbacks for the environment, which is possible only if the working meta program allows for such exceptions, the reality for this listener shifts from "all big manufacturers destroy the environment" to "this manufacturer cares about the community." This is nothing more than a distortion of the filtering system that justifies an emotional state permitted by the meta program driving the whole process. It isn't as much a violation of the filtering criteria as it is a temporary redefinition of them to suit the moment.

Generalization is the casting in stone of the truth—or at least one's personal perception of it—gleaned from personal experience. If in your efforts to be taken seriously by senior management and your peers every proposal and innovative idea you ever presented has been rejected or derided as flawed, you may generalize that all your efforts and initiatives are destined to fail. Your negative experience becomes your truth and thus your filter the next time new information arrives that suggests a possible opportunity for you to contribute value to your organization. The filter of your memories and the ensuing emotional state color the perception of the incoming information—this is a great idea, it could have a positive impact on the way we do business, its implementation will help me gain the respect of my team and senior management—as one with a predestined negative outcome. It is nothing more than a generalization, and if your meta program tells you that you are never wrong about these things and cannot defy your own rules, you'll find a way to sabotage your presentation of ideas or keep from contributing input altogether and settle for watching others shape the business environment in which you operate.

How to Communicate for Maximum Impact and Accurately Transmit the Message

The collective memories, experiences, values, and beliefs of the person to whom you are delivering a message may seem to be a significant hurdle, and rightly so. That means your goal should not be so much to change people's minds as to use their existing thought modeling to your advantage. In other words, the most effective approach is not to challenge the audience but to play to the audience. If you can make your pitch *about them* and the effect that your content will have on their lives rather than *about you* or your priorities, you may be able to bend a belief system that seems less than pliable.

Toward this end you are left with two primary strategies. First, know your audience. Do what you can to understand the way the members of the audience will filter your message, which includes biases and preconceptions that are firmly in place before you utter a word. Go as deep as you can here, working toward an understanding—if not complete acceptance—of the underlying values and belief systems on which those biases and preconceptions are based. The more you speak their language—particularly in terms of context and framing—the better off you'll be when it is time to tell them something that challenges or stretches the status quo.

All this falls into the category of content, and by now we've established that style occupies an equally high place in the hierarchy of effective communication. This means that the nature of your delivery is the second tool you must optimize, including the pace and tone of your words, the nature of your body language, and the visual presentation that packages it all. All five senses are in play here, addressed appropriately in light of what you know about your audience, your team, or the higher-level executives whose perceptions of you play a major role in your professional advancement.

In baseball, the effectiveness of a pitch is as much about placement and spin as it is about power, and the best pitchers in the game study opposing hitters ahead of time. The same is true for our business, political, and personal pitches, which may or may not be headed for the sweet spot of the audience. However, with the right timing and delivery and with spin that optimizes your chances because you've done your homework, you'll have given your message the best shot it can have at success.

In Chapter 2 we'll discuss how you can develop your social IQ, on which most of your success as a respected communicator and leader will ride.

PART II

INFLUENCING PEOPLE AND EVENTS: THE FOUNDATION FOR SUCCESS IN COMMUNICATION

2

Developing Your Social Intelligence

MANY PEOPLE BELIEVE that success depends less on *what* you know than on *who* you know. Although it continues to define the culture of professions such as consulting and making movies, the technocreep of the last three decades has proved the reverse to be equally true: You don't need to know a soul if your idea is some combination of timely and hot and if it pencils out on an Excel spreadsheet. Since 1990 the Internet has spawned more millionaires, each with an evolved entrepreneurial digital sensibility, than Merrill Lynch and Amway combined did in their heyday. Often, thanks to the solitary miracle of e-mail, not even a handshake has been involved.

Lately there's been a third element in this career-ascent mix, and it's getting some serious ink thanks to a bumper crop of utterly clueless corporate executives who seem to have insulated themselves in steel towers of their own making while losing touch with the very people they are supposed to lead or to whom they're pitching their vision. What they haven't realized yet is that yesterday's dog-eat-dog, Marie Antoinette management sensibility went out of style with Jack Welch's office furniture.

Today's generation of managers is realizing that nice guys don't necessarily finish last, that in fact being anything other than socially sensitive and evolved—whether it's a genuine or a strategic agenda—can get you a seat at a congressional hearing and a few heavy-handed punch lines from Jon Stewart.

This mysterious new requisite for managerial success and the attention of the C-suite is called *social intelligence,* and if you think it has any substantive connection to the analytical and reasoning skills that get a person a Mensa card, think again.

At a glance it might seem that social intelligence is synonymous with or at least a subset of *emotional* intelligence, itself a relatively recent take on the controversial belief that *intelligence* is only a global term that refers to the sum of various and discrete human capabilities. However, the term *social intelligence* is much older than the 1980s revolution of thought that the unveiling of emotional intelligence concepts spawned. It first was used by the Columbia University psychologist Edward Thorndike in a 1920 article for *Harper's Monthly Magazine* in which he explained that "the best mechanic in a factory may fail as a foreman for lack of social intelligence." Some 80 years later, when the consultant Karl Albrecht and the writer and Harvard psychologist Daniel Goleman put forth the theory of social intelligence as a context separate from its cousin emotional intelligence, we understand the difference between the two. Who hasn't seen examples such as a promising sales rep who has been promoted to sales manager only to trip over her lower lip with complete and utter ineptitude?

Social Intelligence versus Emotional Intelligence

Emotional intelligence is one's understanding and even mastery of one's own reactions and feelings. When a recently hired executive actually understands why she is having difficulty adapting to the new culture, for example, she may have achieved a high level of emotional intelligence, whereas those who have no clue why they're being passed over for the lead on team projects may run short on EQ, despite the fact that they can whip through a Rubik's cube in less than a minute. When someone with anger issues learns how to control his temper, this is emotional intelligence at work. Clearly, as with other forms of intelligence, the more, the better, and when this type of intelligence is abundant, the chances of navigating away from the inherent consequences of one's issues increase vastly. Executives who have a perfectionist attitude but are learning to set priorities to keep projects moving, for example, exhibit high emotional intelligence because they have mapped the internal landscape of their emotions, allowing them to weigh both impulse and consequence with a healthy perspective.

With emotional intelligence it's all about your own issues, the internal landscape of your psyche; that means that if you stop there, you haven't seized the inherent opportunity that can be found in optimizing the way you are perceived by others. Perception is not so much about what's inside you as it is about what you put out there that determines that perception.

Social intelligence is not an inward awareness, though it's tough to master if you aren't in touch with your inner landscape (emotional intelligence) to some extent. It is very much about how you are perceived by others or, better put, the *management* of what will be perceived by others. It is the understanding—and, when you get it right, the mastery— of what elicits a response from other people in both relationships and casual encounters and even in front of an audience full of strangers. Why is it that some managers get people to line up behind them with staunch to-the-death loyalty, whereas others remain the butt of cruel water cooler banter and reluctant hierarchical deference masquerading as respect? The answer is social intelligence: The first type of manager has it, and the second doesn't. If the second one somehow has risen to the position of boss—though this is more and more unlikely in today's business culture— everyone has a problem.

Social intelligence can be as simple as knowing that a smile and the remembering of a name align with attraction and loyalty much more than do a scowl and a limp handshake regardless of how well a person executes the job description. Social intelligence is not just a buzzword; it's an entire spectrum of survival skills that can make the difference in a career.

Clearly, social intelligence is not the sole defining element in success. There are, after all, many legends of famously cantankerous yet charismatic CEOs that indicate that tough guys and even complete jerks can change the world. The half-full view of social intelligence, though, contends that the achievements of megalomaniacal, chronically demanding, and socially toxic leaders would have been even more astounding if they had been able to foster loyalty instead of fear. Studies have shown that aggressiveness and stress are not optimally productive states in a neurological sense, yet even brilliant tyrants succeed, perhaps in spite of themselves.

How did our long list of legendary corporate Napoleons succeed? Again, social intelligence is not the entire ball game. There are multiple aspects in the academia of intelligence, or so the theory goes: abstract and cognitive intelligence that leads to quick and accurate reasoning and deduction, practical intelligence that empowers people to accomplish goals, aesthetic intelligence that takes the form of artistic expression and appreciation, kinesthetic intelligence that explains why certain people can do things with a ball that you cannot and why some people are naturals at flying airplanes and doing brain surgery, emotional intelligence that empowers self-aware people, and social intelligence, which can trump them all if it allows others to perceive a person as a leader, as someone worthy of getting their attention, and offers an opportunity to take the helm. Think of these as cards in a deck; we are all dealt different hands. Some people, though only for a while, can get by with a good bluff—there are numerous dethroned politicians and CEOs in jail to prove this point—and others toss in their cards and try to improve their lot. However, when you are called out, what you are holding ultimately defines you and creates your path.

It is no longer enough to be intelligent in the cognitive sense. Minimum-security penitentiaries—so-called country clubs for white-collar criminals—are full of intelligent people. Some brilliant people sleep under bridges. It is also not enough to be emotionally intelligent. A doctor being judged on bedside manner, a hostage negotiator, a trial lawyer, a field sales rep, an organization's leader, an executive coach—all are defined as much by their social intelligence as by any other realms of intelligence, including the emotional kind. The book *The Smartest Guys in the Room* proved that its title was nothing short of stupendously ironic when many of the Enron executives who starred in it ended up disgraced and behind bars.

Some define social intelligence as a matter of demonstrating good *people skills*. This is like saying that John Updike had a way with words or that Josh Groban can carry a tune. It would be more accurate to say that social intelligence is a *sense* of the energy and image one is putting out to others, coupled with an understanding of what works and what doesn't, what will cultivate loyalty and approval and what will come off as egotistic, insecure, and insensitive. Social intelligence is more than getting along—it's about getting ahead—with people. If your job is to lead, to sell, to convince, to appeal, to build a culture, to create a following, to sell yourself as an essential aspect of meeting your goals, social intelligence becomes the centerpiece of your skill set. The attainment of your goals depends on it no matter how well you know your stuff otherwise.

Another way to view social intelligence is to consider it the differentiator between the masses and the high achievers. The masses in this context are your peers in your profession or avocation. If you are a doctor, you are surrounded by brilliant peers, many of whom want the chief of surgery spot just as much as you do. Whatever you do, chances are that everyone in the lunchroom is possessed of high intelligence in terms of cognitive skills and the ability to get his or her head around the mechanics of the job, and if the job involves motor skills, everyone in the vicinity has the kinesthetic ability to get it done. General intelligence in this regard is simply the ante, and unless you use your social intelligence to set yourself apart and become a candidate for leadership because people are attracted to you and will line up behind you, you'll remain mired among those intelligent masses.

Breaking Down Social Intelligence

Executives looking to command the respect of their peers and superiors must remember that social intelligence (SI) involves a lot more than an infectious grin and the endearing tendency to slap people on the back. SI is the confluence of a handful of distinct abilities, all of them driven by a keen understanding of what makes people respond. Even if you get along with everyone and are the first person people think of when composing their invitation lists, you owe it more to these five dimensions (as defined by Karl Albrecht) of social intelligence than to your razor-sharp wit.

Presence

What used to be called dressing for success has come out of the closet to include the totality of your presentation across all the senses (the stuff of perception), from your hair to your voice, your movements, and the subtle ways in which you respond. Your presence communicates your self-worth and confidence as well as the level of respect you have for others and the occasion. Disrespect in the name of "just being who I am" gets you nowhere in the world of employers, peers, and clients.

Clarity

Anyone who has ever had a manager, regardless of how nice he or she was, who couldn't communicate objectives, expectations, and specific information clearly knows that it's hard to follow that kind of leader. The goal is to get others to appreciate you and follow you, and the clearer you are about what you want and expect, the sooner that will happen. Competence is one of the most attractive things we humans can cultivate as long as we don't dress it up with arrogance and ego.

Awareness

Awareness is the ability to read people and the moment (think of it as social radar) and respond with behaviors that fit the situation. Upon meeting the first lady, you don't say, "Hey, what's up?" though this might be exactly what you'd say when meeting the 16-old-son of your CEO.

Authenticity

If awareness is your social radar, authenticity is playing to the social radar of others by being genuine, honest, and respectful. Phoniness and bluster, no matter how proficiently conveyed, are easy to spot and consistently off-putting on several levels. They convey a sense of insecurity, which is not what others seek in a leader, and are unpleasant to be around, which is not what you want when you are cultivating the loyalty of others. The concept of honesty goes beyond telling the truth; it embraces conveying the truth about *yourself* as well.

Empathy

Dale Carnegie was on to something when he taught that the more we show a genuine interest in others, the more they'll be attracted to us. Social intelligence takes this a step further than showing interest; we also need to *empathize* with the experience and feelings of others, to *relate* to it and to them. When you communicate empathy, you are saying that we are on the same page, the same team, and that anything I ask you to do has taken your situation into consideration and I have confidence that you can accomplish the goal even though it's difficult.

All this may sound a lot like emotional intelligence until you recognize the context of outbound expression as opposed to inward introspection. It is one thing to manage your emotions, control your temper, disassociate from unpleasant memories and biases, and quell the inner voices of insecurity when you are standing in the spotlight. Social intelligence, in contrast, is the way you manage those things in the context of the way you interface with others, the way you optimize the perception of others with the only element of that perception you can control: the raw input of what people sense about you. From there they will filter that incoming information in ways over which you have no control. Their personal filter is beyond your reach, and it consists of preferences and biases and their own agendas and memories, among other things, which may or may not make sense to you.

The Seven Keys to Social Intelligence

There's an old Steve Martin joke: "How do you avoid paying taxes on a million dollars? Well, first you get a million dollars." In other words, knowing how social intelligence breaks down into its component parts is only the first step in raising your social IQ above where it is today.

Actually changing behaviors, especially one's own, is a monumental undertaking; that is why most professionals embarking on that process appreciate the fact that there is a model in place to get them there. It can be accomplished in seven days, and the process springs from focusing on the components that define social intelligence in the first place.

How to Boost Your Social Intelligence Quotient in Only Seven Days

You can develop your social intelligence, but it requires a keen sense of self, including the honest feedback of others, to assess your starting point and the areas in which you need the most work. Think of social intelligence as the point guard of your game, with the other dimensions of your intelligence ready to win the game once you've aligned others with your goals and recruited a loyal following. Without the latter you become something of an intellectual free agent, and unless you are a poet or a night watchman, your career will suffer.

One way to obtain quality feedback is to conduct a *360-degree assessment* of the way you are perceived by others. That term comes from the places where feedback is solicited: literally all around you, including above and below. This means that you will be reviewed by peers at various levels of daily proximity: those who work for and under you and those to whom you report, as well as the bosses of your boss. The more input from a variety of directions you receive, the better informed you'll be about how you're coming off in a social and a professional context. In the absence of a formal 360-degree review system, you can solicit this input on your own. However you do it, make sure to use the results productively to define what you need to improve about your social intelligence and what is working well.

What follows is not dissimilar to a diet that delivers basic biochemical science instead of fads and marketing agendas. Can you lose weight in seven days? Certainly. Can you change your life and keep the weight off after those seven days? Only if what you've learned during those days becomes a lifestyle. The same thing holds true here. If you can get your head around these concepts in the first seven days, chances are that you'll notice a change in the way people react to you and, more important, at least if it's working, a change in the way you react to other people and the way that makes you feel.

Day 1: Start Using Your Senses More Deliberately

Begin the practice of really using your senses instead of relying on autopilot when you are moving through the day. For instance, when you drive to work, you may not notice many of the sights along the way; you just arrive at work without having given much thought to the environment, architecture, and landscape along the way. If asked, chances are that you couldn't describe any one of them in much detail. Try this the next time you drive to work in your car or on the subway. Simply take a good look around you. Take notice of people's moods in other cars or on the sidewalk. Check out their clothing, note any peculiarities, and try to assign meaning to what you see. Notice the businessman who eats an egg salad sandwich on the way to work in the morning on the subway, impeccably dressed but with crumbs landing on his tie. Notice the old lady cradling a toddler in her arms. Is it her granddaughter? A foster child? If you're driving, notice the workers at the construction sites you're passing: Are they young? Older? Try to guess their ethnicity. Open the window and consciously perceive the fleeting smells in the air. What are they? Gasoline? Oil? Heaven from a nearby bakery? Or is someone smoking near where you are? After a while you'll find that you're no longer guessing, that your perceptions are informed with subtle bits of information that lead to quality perceptions and deductions.

Do this with deliberation for the next seven days and notice how it changes your experience. Notice how *present* you are and the way that makes the time richer. For the first five of these days concentrate on one sense: sound, smell, touch, taste, or sight. Start over again on day 6. Choose to perceive consciously as much as you can with one of your senses every day. Become highly attuned to the stimuli entering your field of perception and pay attention to the stories (explanations) you are assigning to what you see. Notice the emotions associated with the experience of your senses. Feel them.

The more you consciously use and experience your senses, the more situational awareness you will gain. After a while, you'll start noticing things that previously escaped you. Bring this skill in the door with you when you arrive at work and you'll already have improved your social intelligence simply by being more aware and perceptive. The result of that will be an improved ability to respond and communicate appropriately and effectively in professional and social situations in the workplace and, not incidentally, when you get home at the end of the day.

Day 2: Critically Assess Your Strengths and Weaknesses

Whether you have Angelina Jolie's looks, Jason Pollock's talent, Donald Trump's self-confidence, or Warren Buffett's knack for choosing smart investments, this is the time to take stock of the good, the bad, and the ugly in yourself. Why? Because to raise your social IQ you have to know what's what and how you stack up against everyone else in the game. Being aware of your strengths not only gives you confidence, it also gives you an opportunity to offer your strengths to others, instantly turning them into fans, if not friends. And what about your liabilities? That's the stuff you wish you had less of—such as the tendency to share too much at the office water cooler, making your peers roll their eyes and resulting in visual feedback that up to this point you've missed, or your resolutions to make it to the gym only to spend half the time you're there chatting and gossiping with the other treadmill flunky.

Use the 360-degree assessment—official or unofficial—to get an idea of your social assets and liabilities. There's a reason people think and feel about you one way or another. Sometimes you'll want to do something about it, and other times you'll write it off as an unshakable belief on their part (CEOs are overpaid, lawyers are greedy, short people have a Napoleon complex, etc.) and decide to do the best you can to sidestep that belief. It's your choice. Either way, though, you're informed and as a result better equipped to enlist their support.

Day 3: Practice Being Authentic

Most of us blend into the vast masses. We hide behind the various masks we wear to put forth our best image. Unfortunately, what gets lost behind the mask is our true self and our real personality, which is the most interesting part of ourselves to other people. For others to feel a connection and trust us, we have to be more authentic. Today you will start by giving people a more honest look at who you really are—the real person behind the mask.

Here's what being authentic and *real* in order to connect with people looks like:

1. Have honest conversations with others about issues and topics that interest you and that matter to you at a deep level.
2. Focus on the objective of building real relationships by having honest and heartfelt conversations.
3. Admit when you're wrong and apologize when you should.
4. Forgive others.
5. Ask for help and offer it to others who could use your help.
6. Take risks by showing your strengths and weaknesses in a public forum.
7. What's interesting about you? Show your unique sides to others.

Start by having more real conversations with the people around you today. See how they respond to the real you. Observe how much of your true self people feel comfortable with and adjust the amount you want to share. Pick the right time to open yourself up, since too much too soon or out of the context of the moment will lead to the wrong perception. Observe whether people respond with self-disclosure of their own, whether they too become more *real* around you. Take the cue from them and ease into a more profound inter-action with those with whom you want to connect.

Day 4: Start Communicating Simply

Communicate with clarity by using simple English. Make your messages clear and to the point, devoid of complexity and jargon. If you find your-self using complex language and unnecessary details for the purpose of masking your perceived insecurities, stop yourself short and recognize that your new, evolved social intelligence is kicking in. You may be surprised at how often you do this, and when you stop doing it, you may be surprised at how much better the response will be.

Day 5: Practice Empathy: Look at Everything from Someone Else's Perspective

Adopt another person's point of view. Really put yourself into that person's shoes and imagine what it—whatever "it" is—feels like for him or her.

We humans see and experience the world from our own perspective. We filter information through our own unique set of values, beliefs, and biases, and that leads to a concluding perception and a corresponding response. Seeing the world through eyes other than our own will give us a better idea of what's important to others and what moves them, what motivates them to work with us. When we can see their perspective clearly and demonstrate empathy, we can start communicating in a way that appeals to their unique path of filtering. Doing this puts people at ease and breaks down barriers of mistrust and feelings of distance and strangeness. In trying to get us to understand them, people often say, "Look at it from my point of view" or "Here's where I'm coming from." These statements simply ask us to do things that would make for better relationships and increased understanding, and it's more effective if they don't have to ask.

Day 6: Practice Listening with Empathy

When we communicate with a person, we often think about what we're going to say as that person is speaking to us. Our eyes drift, we tune the person out, and more often than not the person notices that and assigns meaning to it.

As a result we miss important pieces of information, cues, nuance, and meaning, not to mention coming off as aloof and disinterested. We fail to establish a real connection when we are not listening because our body language is not fully attuned to the other person's message and our responses are slightly off, consisting of ritualistic grunts, head movements, and hollow nodding. If your feedback tells you that this is you, your social intelligence needs a booster shot.

As you listen to others, consciously put your values, biases, needs, and preferences aside and try to sense empathically what your partner thinks, feels, needs, and perceives, right there in that very moment, and do it without judgment. When appropriate, periodically acknowledge the other person's communication; that acknowledgment can be verbal, vocal, or nonverbal, with sincere eye contact and/or within a few words. Be fully *present*. Observe what your partner does, how the two of you are engaged in way that connects you. Observe in yourself how it feels to perceive fully and get all of a person's communication signals, many of which reside between and behind the actual words.

Day 7: Make a Plan and Implement the Steps

As you're reading this book, you've most likely made the decision to construct or improve your executive presence. Gaining the respect of your peers is a marathon, not a sprint. Although these seven days are just the beginning of a long stretch, you'll have a much clearer idea of what it means to have a vastly improved social IQ. Now it's time to create a plan for you to practice and implement these steps. If you work and communicate with others on a regular basis, you'll have plenty of opportunities to practice these techniques, all of which will take you forward in your career and in your personal relationships.

Chapter 3 will help you read people and predict their behavior, another critical part of increasing your social intelligence.

3

How to Read People and Predict Behavior

THERE'S AN EXPRESSION that often is used when a person wants to avoid full accountability: "I know enough to be dangerous." It's a terrific way to get off the hook when someone wants you to undertake a task you know you have no business tackling—cooking dinner for twelve, doing your own taxes, talking someone down off a ledge—and it feels a lot better than copping to complete ignorance. However, too often we don't apply this gambit when we absolutely should, rendering the expression more clever than useful. For example, most of us believe that we're pretty good at reading people, that is, assigning meaning to subtle gestures and body language. We believe we know, for example, that when people have their arms crossed, they're closed and defensive; that having the hands on the hips means a stand is being taken, perhaps tinged with aggression; and that casting one's eyes to the heavens means that something is being considered.

For executives who spend most of their waking hours interacting with and leading others so that they can meet any number of business objectives, a merely peripheral understanding of body language is as woefully insufficient as a flight simulator is when it constitutes a pilot's only practical experience. To gain the respect and executive presence that leadership requires, a deeper understanding of the art and science of reading people is imperative. The fact is that much of what we believe about body language is a myth—research shows that people are only 20 percent efficient in reading body language—and that to sense the true meaning in visual, verbal, and nonverbal clues we should rely on much more complex analysis and a host of other variables.

It all begins with a simple technique that very few people are consciously aware of. However, without that fundamental skill, what you think you see may not be what you get.

Human Message Decoding: An Entry-Level Primer

What we see—even what we hear—is only the tip of a very complex and often immovable psychological iceberg. To open this examination of how to read the people around us, we begin by looking at a terrifying phenomenon that we experience each and every day: the driver from hell. What that driver is doing—and not doing—mirrors the way many people conduct their lives, and it defines the difference between astute people readers and those who see only the obvious.

We've all ridden with this person or, just as frightening, found ourselves in the lane next to him. It's the driver who operates a car as if there were some sort of factory-installed autopilot device involved, the one who pays more attention to the e-mail on her BlackBerry than to the road or thumbs an iPod while merging onto a rush hour freeway, the woman applying makeup in the rearview mirror while changing lanes, the curmudgeon who believes he holds the deed to the fast lane—it's his world; you just happen to be driving in it—and doesn't feel much like hurrying today.

We've all been there. Although these drivers account for a preponderance of accidents, both minor and catastrophic, it's amazing that there aren't even more fender benders and fatalities what with the sheer mass of the autopilot demographic that behaves this way.

It's also amazing how many people live their entire lives this way. The germane question here is this: Are these people even remotely paying attention? Are they even seeing the road in front of them? The answer is yes; they couldn't keep their cars between the lines if nothing in their field of vision registered in some part of their distracted brains. It truly is an autopilot of sorts; they are relying on instincts and learned responses, just like the whales jumping through hoops at Sea World. For the most part, other than a few horns and meaningful gestures, it gets them safely, albeit cluelessly, to their destination. They manage, they get by, and it never occurs to them that other people have to compensate for their behavior.

If they're seeing what they need to see to survive the ride, what's the problem, and what does this have to do with reading people and their behavior, and what, if any, impact does it have on the career of someone who is on the way up the corporate ladder? To answer this question, consider the many clues we may be missing in our associates during critical negotiations in which we work out the details of a contract with a business partner and make concessions we're not sure we had to make to close the deal or when we present an idea to the board and miss a crucial sign of discontentment from a key member that would have allowed us to adjust course and address the issue immediately instead of letting it fester and become the focus of discussion behind closed doors later. Although it may be fine to just get by when driving a car, the reason you're reading this book is that you want to be in control of how others see you and the decisions you make—decisions that are based on astute observation as opposed to going through the motions—to establish the kind of presence that others will respect.

The ultimate key to the driving metaphor, the insight that will allow you to read other people in a way that really does empower you, is this: Although they may be *seeing* the road, these drivers are not *observing* the road. Better stated, they're not *taking in all the available data*, the clues and potential variables surrounding them, and certainly aren't assigning any meaning to the data. Airline pilots call this process of observation and analysis *situational awareness*, and you can bet your frequent flier miles they're not putting on eyeliner or making prolonged eye contact with the copilot while operating a 300-ton aircraft. Rather, they are observing anything and everything, using both human and electronic means, and assigning significance and playing out options for every combination of variables that registers. Through observation—and only through observation—they are aware of what *could* happen and can differentiate it from what *might* happen long before the moment of inevitability arrives. Precisely because of what they've observed, they're already creating a management plan that includes a proactive, objectives-driven response for both possibilities.

The pilot, unlike the distracted driver, is observing and decoding everything in sight with a view toward optimizing an outcome. You, as a professional with a flight plan for your career, can and should do the same thing in your world. How? By observing and reading the people around you and then assigning meaning and formulating possible responses by decoding what you see and what you sense.

Basic Instinct: Values and Criteria That Define What Matters

What do we mean by reading another person? It's as simple as knowing that someone is upset with just one glance—married people quickly master this—or sensing that you are out of the loop from the way others in a group are behaving. Many people can walk into a room and within moments sense the tone and tenor, allowing them to adjust their demeanor appropriately.

The reading of another person is truly a sum that exceeds its parts. Those parts include *what* people say (words and implications of words), *how* they say it (volume, tone, nuance), their body language while saying it, and, among many other variables perhaps the most important, the *context* of it all. For the truly astute, people reading isn't just the noticing of clues; two people can observe the same circumstances and draw completely different conclusions, and usually only one of them is right.

Before any conclusions can be reached, incoming observations are filtered and processed; by definition, this adds the internal and highly personal variables of bias, memory, urgency, agenda, fear, paranoia, and a whole litany of other psychological influences to the conclusion-making machine. In other words, the receiver has as much to do with perception—we've discussed this in detail in the first chapter—as does the roster of clues and implications resulting from the verbal and non-verbal clues that person observes. Truly advanced people readers take this into consideration and strive to objectify their conclusions by factoring in the filter of their own worldview.

There is a trap called the *false consensus bias:* the tendency to apply one's values and choices to others. Simply put, if people choose and behave as we do or in a way we approve of, if they have our values and belief systems, they are okay—and vice versa. Enlightened executives know that engineers view the world one way, and marketing executives another. They know that accounting, sales, and manufacturing often have decidedly different values that, if ignored, can lead to gridlock, delays, and derailment in meetings and discussions in which consensus is the goal. At the center of it all, in addition to bias, is a misunderstanding of the motives of people who don't share your view, which frequently can lead to hostile and aggressive responses.

It is a very human trait, one that evolved people readers understand and work to circumvent. They do that by mastering the tools of the trade.

Mastering Values and Criteria Analysis to Find Out What Matters Most to Someone Else

In the study of people reading, one always must keep the ultimate goal in mind. The whole point is to optimize an outcome rather than to judge others. In sales this means understanding what the prospect really needs and what her potential objections are and tailoring your pitch to fit those variables. With your boss you need to avoid hot buttons and predict the standards of successful performance. You need to pick your moments and tailor your verbal and nonverbal broadcasts. All these things require some degree of the ability to read moods, sensing levels of stress or distraction, gauging the extent of openness and the level of risk of opening a can of worms, and otherwise saying and doing the right thing at the right time— not so much for you as for them. The more data you observe toward these ends and the more astute you are in not allowing your personal filters to cloud the truth—*their* truth—the more effective and empowered you'll be in reading people and situations accurately.

Some people proudly proclaim that they say what they feel, when they feel it, without regard to the other person. They're "just being honest," the consequences be damned. Perhaps, but are they reading those around them accurately with a view to optimizing an outcome? Probably not. Certainly, they aren't always optimally productive with their self-proclaimed insensitivity. In fact, their behavior delivers a set of data that is observed and perceived by others, and those perceptions come to bear on their lives in dark ways that more astute people readers can avoid.

Take an employment interview as an example. Bosses come in all flavors in terms of values, demeanor, and expectations. Some prioritize the working environment and personal growth for employees; they are all about company culture and family. Others are all about productivity and the numbers: Go tell your troubles to someone who cares. Some are goal-driven and give people the latitude to do what needs doing; others are procedural control freaks who go totally by the book. The interviewee who pitches his own perspective without some sense of where the interviewer sits on these issues risks immediate alienation. Those who can read the interviewer with a view toward what is valued are empowered to tailor their presentation and demeanor accordingly. It isn't so much about becoming something you aren't; it's about avoiding pitfalls and playing to your strengths in the areas you perceive to be important to the person sitting in front of you. For that to happen, you need to be able to read that person.

To accomplish this, to become a true people reader beyond the level of intuitive perceptiveness most people possess, you must follow a process that has two basic elements: the observation and gathering of data, which includes knowing what to look for and what it means, and understanding how your personal filters may distort the true and useful meaning of that data and then adjusting your perceptions and decisions accordingly.

On the second aspect of the process, it's easy to see that a person who clings to certain biases can distort what is true or at least what is productive. For example, do you view smokers as people with an addiction or as people with a character flaw? Do you believe that people who drive hybrid cars have less profit-driven ambition than do those who drive German imports? Do you believe Asians and Indians are more analytical and technically astute (cultural barriers and biases are one of the strongest contaminants of objective people reading)? Do you think that people who swear are intellectually or socially different from people who don't? Do people who avoid eye contact have personal issues? Are they lying to you? Do people who opt for designer clothes have a self-image different from that of those who aren't fashion-forward? Does an applicant who appears nervous fare differently than one who is casual and friendly? Do people who are poor tippers make more astute and conservative financial professionals?

The list of potential biases and meanings is astoundingly long, and all the perceptions and conclusions that spring from it are dependent more on the filters of the observer than on the individual doing the broadcasting of the data. Two people can have the exact same answers to the same questions yet assign to those answers diametrically opposite meanings from which opposite responses are made manifest. Only by taking yourself out of the equation can you assess accurately what is important to the other person, which is the key to harnessing the power of reading people. That balance—what is important to them and what is important to you—becomes the formula by which you compute your decisions and behaviors toward others.

Notice that I'm not suggesting that you set aside what you value; instead, you should work toward not letting it affect your assessment of what the other person values. If either side of the filtering process is skewed, the perception process will be compromised.

Factors That Make It Difficult to Read and Interpret Other People's Attitudes and Behavior and How to Get around Them

Reading people is always a chancy process. There are myriad ways to contaminate that process, and only through an awareness of their lurking presence can you work around them to achieve objectivity and comprehensiveness.

We've all been surprised by the realization that our first impression of a person turned out to be wrong. We misread the clues gathered through our initial observation, and only as a result of continued exposure to that person can we gather more data and realize that this was a book that could not be judged by its cover. *Time* is an empowerer of people reading; if you have it, take care not to cast your initial impressions in stone.

Once you know people well, it's easier to read them. This is the case because you are able to establish a *baseline* for a person: what's normal for that person without any discernible issues or pressures coloring his or her behavior. Someone may be naturally quiet to the extent that others perceive her as aloof or without passion, but you may know otherwise, and that means the data you gather begin with an established baseline (that person is, by nature and without much significance, quiet) that is credible. You know this person's patterns, and so even the slightest deviation registers. You know that his habitual slouching doesn't really mean he is aloof and disinterested; it's just the way he situates himself in a chair (this is the risk of buying into the myth of body language). You know that a woman's habit of interrupting people doesn't mean she is self-centered and uninterested; it's just a quirk that she may or may not need to work on.

By using the baseline, you can challenge and refine your assumptions and conclusions and make a decision that is based on data and thus is less dependent on your filters and biases. Although someone else may dismiss the person because of all the interruptions, you know that if you ask her to shut up and listen, she will do so.

These four steps—establishing a baseline, recognizing patterns, challenging and refining your assumptions, and then drawing a conclusion— are the fundamental principles of reading people. The better you know someone, the more valid the model becomes, because with strangers and casual acquaintances the baseline by definition is one of your own making, derived from your own distorting beliefs, biases, and experiences.

Pitfalls of Perception versus Windows of Observation

As you are crafting your executive presence, be aware that the most common hitch in the people-reading process is *faulty observation*, of which you may be a target as well as a practitioner. We make conclusions regardless of the quality of the observation and filtering process, and so the objective is to optimize those processes to ensure the integrity of the conclusion. If we don't gather all the data, if we simply see instead of notice, if we're too busy talking to listen, we revert to the less sensitive instinctual mode of observation that links more directly to bias and judgment than does truly observed behavior within the context of informed analysis.

Another trap is the human tendency to notice and perhaps overweigh *negative* observations. This one stems from the deepest recesses of our DNA, which programs us to react to danger in self-preserving ways; what that means is that we are assigning relevance to what we observe. Negative emotions are contagious; they trigger our fears or paranoia. In fact, they trigger an actual physiological response that cements them in a person's consciousness. Research shows that we are more keenly attuned to the negative energy of others; that means that as evolved and astute people readers, we must proactively open ourselves to positive data that otherwise might be deemed less relevant.

Part of recognizing that we may be filtering incoming data inaccurately is the awareness of our own *mood*. We've all had days when we love everyone and the world is a beautiful place—that means we are tuned to the positive energies around us—and days when we'd rather be alone because nothing or nobody is clicking. Your mood should be the first thing you assess when you are filtering information, making sure that you aren't coloring the incoming data with your frustrations or feelings.

One useful window of data is the environment within which someone insulates himself, including his workspace, his clothing, and even his car. Again, the better you know the person, the more useful the data are, because this is an easy area in which to overgeneralize. Does a luxury car signify the need for status or show that the person inherited a bunch of money? Does driving an old gas guzzler instead of a small import mean the person is cavalier and elitist or that she can't afford a newer model? Does a cluttered desk mean a person is disorganized or simply busy? Does the presence of plants and flowers have significance, or is it the person's birthday? The trick is to avoid generalization and use these observations as raw data, which are most effective when bundled and shaped to work productively within your objective filtering process.

A less obvious pitfall is called the *halo effect*: the tendency to assume that because someone is viewed with approval in one area, by default he gets the benefit of the doubt in other areas. This is a form of bias that like any other bias clouds the data-filtering process and may lead to an inaccurate or unproductive outcome. Back in school, was your teacher always right or, more germane to this discussion, always righteous? Were your parents perfect? Did they walk on water, meaning that all their values were virtuous? For some of us, did their flaws negate areas of wisdom we otherwise might have discounted? How about our political candidates? Does their party affiliation make all their decisions sound and their platforms reasonable? In the 2008 Ron Howard film *Frost/Nixon*, during which the dethroned president is interviewed by the television talk show host David Frost, Nixon is asked, "So are you really saying that the president can do something illegal?" To which he answers, "I'm saying that when the president does it, that means it's *not* illegal." This is the halo effect in full elitist glory, not only in terms of the perception of others but as license for someone to do as he sees fit regardless of the perception of others.

The halo effect also affects the perception of simple likability. When a sports hero speaks at a high school assembly, he is accepted and liked by the students instantly regardless of his rap sheet or the number of weapons hidden in the trunk of his Mercedes. Same thing for authors, artists, actors, politicians, and anyone else with a public persona of accomplishment; the halo precedes them and affects the perceptions of everyone on both a conscious and an unconscious level. Astute people readers recognize this and are able to see beyond the glow of the halo to assess what they observe objectively and then use the data to make informed and productive decisions.

Another pitfall is called *disconfirmation bias*, and it connects to one's personal worldview and value system. This trap snaps shut when we easily accept what we perceive as correct and strongly believe in and rigorously scrutinize or reject outright that which we consider false or wrong. An example would be a member of a board of directors enthusiastically embracing a new CEO candidate upon learning of that executive's qualifications and experience but working strenuously to reject the candidate after learning about her alternative lifestyle. If we believe strongly in something, we often accept it quickly and easily and without deeper analysis, yet if some or all of it reveals a conflict with our values and beliefs, we find a way to make it wrong, using orders of magnitude more energy in the effort. This assessment of right or wrong is biased from the outset rather than being the result of objective filtering. What this means to us is that when faced with others who bring a disconfirmation bias to their filtering process, we must bring overwhelming and incontrovertible evidence to our side of an argument to overcome their initial and often subconscious tendency to discount what we believe.

Similar to disconfirmation bias is the *selective exposure* phenomenon. In this case we tend to avoid information, people, and situations that conflict with our attitudes and worldview—our way of thinking. The larger the gap, the more intense our efforts to avoid exposure. An example would be a manager who will limit his research on a new computer system for the department to a certain brand or manufacturer, avoiding any information from competitors that might threaten his preference for the original choice. Executives looking to increase their professional presence in the workplace need to recognize this pitfall by introducing new information carefully when trying to influence others on issues that conflict with a firmly held attitude.

Another factor that influences perception is the *actor/observer difference*. This is the tendency to assign the actions and traits of people to their personalities—that's just the way they are—while explaining and justifying our own behavior as an informed response to situations and opportunities. You may view someone who refuses to make an investment in a company you believe in as fearful and overly conservative, whereas you view yourself as prudent and a student of the market. The opportunity here for astute people readers resides in realizing that they may be viewing you by using the same actor/observer difference. In this example that means you're viewed as a risk-taking, impulsive thinker, whereas they view themselves as someone who simply has assessed the situation and has decided the risks outweigh the upside. This awareness becomes the baseline from which you can tailor your approach to optimize results by speaking from the other person's perspective instead of your own.

This is similar to what is known as *attribution theory*. In using this model, you may explain others' actions and behaviors as resulting from internal factors, such as fear or ignorance, whereas your decisions are the result of external factors such as proximity and available input. Both are self-justifications that color the other person's view with a shade of reality different from your own, always a dangerous variable when trying to maximize your communications with others.

To the extent that these variables are affecting your communications, they are most likely subconscious, leaving the management of them to your ability to recognize and overcome. All of them drive toward the goal of objectifying the way you filter information, and the success of the process depends on your ability to understand how your beliefs, biases, and worldview may be affecting your perceptions and your understanding of the needs of others. Turning the communications process inside out—from the perspective of what you want to what the other party wants—empowers your ability to use people-reading skills productively.

Putting It All in Play: How the FBI Reads People

It's fair to say that the higher the stakes are, the more people expose their thoughts, goals, and character in nonverbal ways and through the style and tone of their verbal communications. Speechmaking, employment interviews, performance reviews, and executive coaching sessions designed to correct toxic behavior—or boost performance—are all important and stressful, but they pale in comparison to what happens within the gray walls of a federal interview room when you are staring into the inquisitive eyes of a seasoned FBI investigator whose job it is to sweat the truth out of you. They do that through the astute application of the same people-reading techniques we have been discussing in this chapter. Executives who strive to manage the perceptions of their peers would do well to adopt some of the following people-reading strategies.

Experienced investigators know that body language provides clues to the truthfulness or validity of the spoken word, though they go far beyond the shallow myths most people use. Eye contact is a major issue: Liars actually increase the frequency of eye contact in a misguided effort to create the impression of sincerity. This dispels the myth of avoidance linking to the masking of truth, and it is something that astute people readers should understand.

They also watch the movement of the eyelids during interrogations. People in disagreement or disapproval tend to close their eyes longer than a normal blink. This is useful when you have an established baseline with someone, because you will notice an altered blinking pattern during a discussion in which the facts or outcome is in dispute.

This is the reason federal agents try to do interviews with a minimum of visual interference between them and the subject. The desk is barren, or if they are not in their own environment, they'll try to question the subject away from a desk or in a place where they can observe the entire person as he gives his answers. With body language, the more body you can see, the better.

Context is another variable that expert interrogators understand and that an astute people reader always should consider. Stress places physical and emotional demands on people, and altered or aberrant behavior may result as much from how they're reacting to the moment as from who they are. Both become fodder for analysis, and neither is useful unless you know the difference. The same is true of *comfort* and *discomfort*: These conditions may impart different meanings to body language and other variations of behavior. Only through an understanding of context can you assign meaning accurately.

Professional people readers rely on baseline behaviors to recognize deviations. For them, however, there is very little likelihood of personal familiarity, and so they resort to baseline human behaviors—the norm to look for is signs of squirming or manipulation. This is mitigated by the fact that nearly all their interviews occur in a context of pressure and stress, resulting in a complex mix of adjustments and compensations that other people rarely experience. Nonetheless, those working on their professional presence can benefit greatly by emulating the professionals and the powers of observation they employ, coupled with the processes of filtering and making conclusions.

Like those people, we can benefit from an enlightened understanding of all the principles of astute people reading as we continuously strive to command respect with our executive poise.

In Chapter 4 we'll look at how anyone can learn to get buy-in for his or her ideas and compliance from others for personal and professional success.

4

Engineering Buy-in and Gaining Compliance

THE MILITARY IS on to something and has been since the days of muskets and keelhauling. It goes like this: The brass says, "Jump," and then the troops ask, "How high?" Not only do the enlisted masses not have to like it, those in the higher echelons with the embroidered hats couldn't care less whether they do. In fact, if you're a drill instructor with a bit of a Napoleon complex, the less the grunts like what you tell them to do, the better. The reason this works is obvious: There is no viable alternative. A soldier can't resign. Resistance gets the soldier some quality time in the brig. Request a rationale and you're cleaning the latrine with a tooth-brush—yours—for the next month. The only other situation in modern civilized culture in which this organizational dynamic works is a memory most of us hold dear: When asked to justify an instruction we found illog-ical, which was often the case, our parents said, "Because I said so."

Hence, our generational problems with authority figures.

There was a time in the corporate world when managers who wanted to assert their presence and get to the top of their profession thought that this was the way of the world. Actually, for a time it was, at least until three tough women named Parton, Tomlin, and Fonda rewrote workplace dynamics in the 1980 movie *Nine to Five*, in which the company head played by Dabney Coleman discovers that a title and too much insensitive swagger can get you tied up, literally, in misguided office politics that have significant consequences.

Although the fascist, megalomaniacal styles of middle and upper managers continue to infect the workplace, there's a new cultural sheriff roaming the corporate campus these days, one who's been to all the postgraduate leadership seminars that postulate that people, along with the results they deliver, are best optimized from a specific psychological understanding of what makes them tick. This is a strategy designed for long-term success rather than the short-term benefits of carrying a metaphorical big stick and having an impressive title. When it comes to consequences, nothing says "mission accomplished" more effectively than job descriptions, initiatives, and on-the-fly leadership implemented after a preengineered *buy-in* by the troops.

As a manager or corporate executive, you meet your objectives through the combined skill, talent, and effort of those around you. From colleagues and employees who report to you to the bosses you support with your contributions to the team effort, it is primarily the successful management of human clusters and their individual components that spells success in the corporate world. The way you assert your leadership and get others to do their part will define the way you're perceived by everyone around and above you. There are many ways—hundreds, in fact—to get *compliance*. However, we now know that there are only a few principles of human behavior that generate buy-in, which is the not so elusive magic ingredient that makes long-term sustained organizational success possible. It's the mastery of the concept of buy-in that will generate more respect and honest effort from the members of your greater team—bosses included— and contribute to the executive presence you are learning to build.

Buy-in versus Compliance

Abraham Lincoln said, "Public sentiment is everything. With it, nothing can fail; without it, nothing can succeed." Perhaps the observation originated in the Civil War, in which it's hard to imagine Confederate soldiers shooting up their northern neighbors without buying in to the cultural racial bias that was the crux of the dispute. Johnny Rebel wasn't so much defending his country or even the honor of the South as he was defending a *belief system*, and a belief system is a form of buy-in (if you don't believe, you aren't buying in). Compliance with instructions and defined roles in a culture that is based on a contradictory belief system is destined to fail or at best achieve only the shallowest short-term gains. Imagine Nordstrom instituting a temporary no-return policy in the name of short-term profitability; the result would be the demise of the brand even if profits temporarily soared.

The trick, then, is to sow the seeds of a cultural belief system (such as Nordstrom's uncompromising customer service, Ritz-Carlton's luxurious pampering, McDonald's value, BMW's quality, and Google's creative workplace environment) that underpins all levels of the tasks and roles required to reach a collective goal that is driven by buy-in to a specific set of missions rather than by fear of any consequences that might arise from defiance of the leaders who are requesting or demanding compliance. Compliance without buy-in is always fear-based to some extent—you get to keep your job; this is what will result in a promotion or a raise—and it never achieves fully sustained commitment and effort.

Buy-in, which often is easier to define than to achieve, is an alignment of the thoughts and beliefs of a target demographic with your thoughts and beliefs as the managing or accountable entity. It is a process of working together with people—rather than dictating to them—in a manner that leads to their understanding of the goal and its strategic importance to achieve a win-win outcome, all within a common system of values. It is a matter of gaining people's personal commitment to a goal—as opposed to a fear of failure—and therefore a willingness to undertake and accomplish the necessary tasks and roles. The more complex and significant the project or organizational objective is, the more buy-in becomes an essential component of the strategy to achieve it.

This definition shifts the role of a manager from one of task definer and taskmaster to one of task *empowerer*. Your first line of managerial offense—indeed, your most powerful strategy—is to strive to create a level of buy-in that will accelerate success rather than using compliance and dictatorial power as a doomed and ultimately inefficient means of getting the work done.

The protagonists of the corporate tragedy called Enron are a classic example of the phenomenon of buy-in as well as the lack of it. It's hard to imagine the senior executive team at Enron behaving as they did—and for a time succeeding—without buy-in from lower-ranking executives that was aligned at its moral core—or amoral core, as it were—with the goals of the control-stripped corporation. Once the controls were eliminated—those who questioned unusual accounting practices were laid off—those in power, with the help of those whose buy-in they had, ran rampant in their greed and ran Enron into the ground.

As is often the case when the dust settles and the surviving voices can be heard, we learned that it was the lack of buy-in from several individuals within its culture that helped bring down the corporate giant. They're called whistleblowers, and one Enron whistler—a vice president of corporate development by the name of Sherron Watkins—blew the whistle in CEO Ken Lay's ear in a seven-page letter in which she basically worried aloud about Enron's "funny" accounting practices, likening them to a giant Ponzi scheme. Although Watkins wasn't the only one who didn't buy in—other former Enron executives claimed the title of whistleblower for themselves—she was named person of the week by *Time* magazine for her prolific role in "smelling a rat" at work and documenting it in writing. Watkins and other corporate whistleblowers may have looked the other way here and there—who knows?—but they lacked buy-in to a sufficient degree that they sought to remove themselves from the immoral and unethical, not to mention criminal, activities that doomed the company to failure.

The fact that the greed-laced goals of the Enron leadership did fail, and at great expense to all involved, is the principle of buy-in made palpable: The infrastructure of a corporation infested with illegal accounting practices crumbled in on itself as much for the lack of buy-in among key stakeholders—Watkins for one—as for any other reason.

Imagine a Cinderella-story athletic success without the buy-in of the team. The 1980 American Olympic ice hockey team staffed with college students that beat a team of hard-core professional Soviet players is an example. Imagine a political victory without the buy-in of staff and constituencies. The first victory of an African American for president of the United States is another example. Imagine the superstars of corporate cultural success without across-the-board buy-in to a set of values and values-driven missions. The list of CEOs who achieved this includes Welch, Jobs, and Buffett. The fact is that it is impossible to imagine true team success without buy-in.

Some behaviors and actions—at least behaviors and actions undertaken with full effort and passion over time—cannot be mandated even with a big title and the hammer of a looming performance review. That level of commitment requires buy-in, the kind that permeates all levels of the culture.

Getting Their Attention and Keeping It

Getting the attention of employees as well as peers and top management is easy. Keeping it, as well as harnessing it for the good of the organization, is another matter altogether. The quest for employee performance and results, even when viewed from the lower realm of obedience and passion, comes in two flavors: prosocial and antisocial. Both work, but only one succeeds over the long term, at least if there are no uniforms involved.

A *prosocial* approach is one in which the manager makes a quid pro quo promise along the lines of "You scratch my back and I'll scratch yours." It leverages experience in a way that says that if you do this, I know you'll come out better off when we're done. It offers rewards beforehand and is delivered with a locker room speech and a smile. It comes from the moral high ground—"This is the right thing to do"—and puts power in the hands of the people through an approach that says "I really need your help." If you've earned it, they'll give it to you.

Antisocial management looks completely different. Rather than accompanying a promise, instructions come dressed with a threat: "Do this or you're toast." It forecasts negative outcomes instead of positive ones even if the manager puts himself or herself in the same boat: "Believe me, if we don't get this done, we're all out of a job." The moral—and morale—factor here is one of pressure rather than righteousness:

"Anyone with a sense of responsibility can see that this is a good thing." Also, it sometimes involves calling in a chip: "You owe me from last time."

Prosocial management is all carrots and upside; antisocial management is all pressure and negative consequences. Both will get the troops moving—fear is good for that—but only prosocial approaches allow employees to take their hearts and souls—their personal commitment— with them.

It's hard to imagine a successful coach telling a kicker, "Make this field goal or you're off the team." However, performance milestones and specific employee measurables too are often infused with this subtext without any accompanying positive reinforcement or support on the table. Certainly, employees already understand the need to make the field goal and know that ultimately their place on the roster depends on their ability to score. However, using that as the basis of management is ultimately counterproductive because the employees are not in it for the right reasons, or at least the most productive reasons.

All this boils down to a basic tenet of human behavior: People need a safe and trusting environment. Deep in our DNA there is a voice whispering that if we feel unsafe, we must minimize risk. We need to play it safe if there's a chance we'll end up with our heads on a platter. When this is the case, employees put their energy into the avoidance of risk rather than the creative process of achieving goals, which inherently embraces risk. Only when there is an air of trust flowing through the organization's HVAC system will employees embark on passionate risk taking, which is the ingredient necessary for sustained growth.

Nordstrom serves as a model for this in its aforementioned customer return policy. Workers are empowered to make decisions at the point of contact—to return or not to return. The employees all know that their jobs are safe; regardless of the circumstances, no supervisory approval is required. In fact, the risk occurs when they don't do a return. Although this results in some customers attempting to return shoes bought during the Nixon administration for a full refund, tattered soles and all, the overall effect is a culture of customer service and employee empowerment that serve the brand and make Nordstrom the premier company to work for—and buy from—in the retail clothing market.

The idea here is to create a culture in which decisions are team-driven rather than management-driven. The archaic command-and-control approach is shelved in favor of a culture in which managers admit that they don't have all the answers and will implement and support team decisions. That means managers become the architects of that team dynamic rather than all-seeing purveyors of answers. The result is a culture of trust and employee empowerment that is safe. Employees are not afraid to ask questions and be vulnerable, to request help and suggest changes, to support one another and their manager. They are ready to buy in not only to decisions but to their role in the implementation of those decisions as well.

Here are a few tips to help you get their attention. Remember, the context here is critical. Strive for a prosocial approach lest these ideas be perceived as manipulation rather than cultural empowerment.

- *Shake them up.* Do the unexpected: Call an off-site meeting, bring in food, play music. Be counterintuitive. Generate interest and curiosity, knowing that substance must reside directly beneath the fun and games. You are playing on their turf, not yours. By doing this, you'll be closing the gaps between what they believe and know and what you want them to achieve.
- *Add value.* Attention lasts for only a blink or two, and so you need to seize the moment. They will assess your motives as a knee-jerk reaction, and you must move to inject value so that you will not be perceived as manipulative. One way to do this is to link your approach to the objective in a thematic way, for example, by playing rock music because your project is designed to inject more energy into the customer relationship. Bear in mind that despite your creativity, employees will always bring a what's-in-it-for-me mentality to the moment, so be ready to show them that what you are proposing is a win-win not just for the company and the customer but for them. Most of all, make sure you are doing as much listening as pontificating.
- *Be a storyteller.* Anecdotes are golden in the quest to get attention and recruit buy-in because all stories have a beginning, middle, and end; that equates to goal, action, and

results, all rendered in human terms. When you tell a story, people immediately switch into a different gear that puts business on hold and creates an island of introspection. They will be looking for meaning and a relationship in your shared world, so give it to them in terms that keep them on the edge of their seats. When the outcome promises a rosy future, they immediately will cast themselves into the key roles of the story. We'll talk about this in more detail in Chapter 5.

- *Be human.* Remember the discussion of social intelligence in Chapter 2? It is highly effective in bringing an emotional context to a request for buy-in. The goal is to make employees *feel* your recommendations rather than just hear them. Show how things will change for the better. Make your story a tearjerker to get them to relate to it. Make your pitch personal: Research shows that people are more likely to help a single individual in need than to contribute to a generic charity. Tap into emotional hot buttons just as football coaches post the disrespectful quotes of the other team on the locker room bulletin board.

- *Be the real deal.* Your credibility is always the pivotal variable in terms of how people respond to what you're asking of them. Make sure you're on solid ground, and if you're not, bring the data and the reinforcements necessary to qualify you as their leader. It takes more than a title and a few bags of popcorn; it takes a sense of investment and a true culture of teamwork that leads to a solid win-win proposition.

How People Really Make Decisions: The Role of Human Desire

There's no getting around the fact that managers are dealing with the human animal when they marshal the troops for a mission. The emphasis here is on the word *animal*, which indicates that despite our best intentions and enlightened approach, we are dealing with very basic human needs and emotions. When we understand these drives and default reactions, we are empowered to play to them and overcome them with the compelling logic of our enlightened approach, in other words, to move them toward buy-in.

- *They want to get it right.* As a species people are naturally *pleasers.* Not only do we manage fear and risk to avoid the consequences of failure, we are motivated to look good in the eyes of those who count, and you, as a manager, count. This desire to be right puts pressure on us, and that leads to anxiety. If you know anything about anxiety, you know that this opens the door to all sorts of unproductive states: everything from procrastination, to impulsiveness, to outright panic. Poor decisions are often the product of a sense of anxiety and the feelings of fatigue and being overwhelmed that come with it. Enlightened managers work to mitigate these states by taking anxiety out of the equation. They make the workplace and the process of the mission a safe place to be. The trick is to balance the urgency and stakes of the mission with this state of safety. How? By identifying the specific internal trigger that leads to anxiety. Will the mission result in time pressures and too much evening and weekend work? Will it place the employees in a role in which they feel unprepared or uncomfortable? Will they feel supported in their role or alone with their sense of inadequacy? Are there enough rewards—do they understand what's in it for them? Do the stakes have implications for their careers or their immediate sense of wellness? Sometimes it is impossible to take uncertainty out of the mission, but you can strive to make a state of safety and the availability of support a certainty for the employees to whom you are assigning a role. By allowing the employees to embrace the variables in a safe manner rather than an uncertain one, you are empowering them to buy in.
- *Reduce the playing field.* The sense of being overwhelmed can link to the fact that there are too many available options and choices. This connects to the need to be right and to avoid risk in the face of consequences. Thus, as a manager, your job is to

simplify things not because your people aren't up to facing the complexity but to lessen their sense of fear and anxiety. You are seeking action and boldness, not hesitancy born of the fear of failure, or, as we called it in grad school, analysis paralysis. With multiple options on the table, you should strive for good or even acceptable instead of perfect because the alternative is in fact potential analysis paralysis. KISS shouldn't mean "keep it simple stupid" but "keep it strategically simple."

- *They want it now.* The scientific term for it is *myopia temporal discounting*, and it boils down to this: People will gobble down the dessert even though they know that they'll pay for it with an extra hour in the gym tomorrow. Humans discount future consequences—even potential rewards—in favor of an immediate return, and when we're talking about too many choices and fear of the consequences of hesitancy, they'll jump at the first thing that looks like it could work for them—now. As a manager, your role is to clarify the difference and get them to buy in to future implications rather than leaping after a quick buck.

- *The power of the people.* There is a phenomenon called *social proof* that shows how people will follow the crowd simply to feel that they are a part of it. This is a safety issue and a shortcut to making decisions: If everyone is doing it, if everyone thinks this way, it must be okay, it must be safe. An enlightened manager recognizes this human tendency in devising a strategy to create buy-in and manages around the issues that run contrary to the whims of the crowd. If everyone leaves work at five, social proof says that this is validated as acceptable behavior. In that case a manager will have to target this behavior in a positive manner—prosocial versus antisocial—if longer hours are needed to achieve a goal. Leaving the issue unattended would expose time-sensitive projects and looming deadlines to preexisting paradigms, many of which are cemented by social proof.

As a manager, sometimes you can use these human tendencies to empower your approach; at other times you have to work around them. Either way, they're always in the mix, and buy-in depends on how they are addressed at the outset. If you're working toward creating a leadership presence for yourself—aiming for the role of manager or executive in charge of an entire division—you'll be better prepared to influence your peers if you use the ideas and principles listed above.

How to Inspire and Motivate People for the Long Haul

Google is as famous for its corporate culture as it is for the services it provides, including its de facto association with the art of searching the Web as a verb rather than a noun. This is a place where free goodies abound; there are more perks than executive parking spaces. It is a place where employees become the envy of their friends not because of a paycheck or a piece of the pie but because they get to work in a culture that's creative, energized, and downright fun. A closer look shows how and why this works: None of this cultural nirvana is positioned as a *reward* for performance; it just *is*. Because it just is, employees buy in to the company culture and its mission, and that sets the stage for buy-in to specific strategies and assigned roles.

Google has turned the command and control management paradigm inside out. They haven't created consequences for performance as much as they've created a culture of buy-in that leads to performance. It's all about collaboration, content, and choice (what Alfie Kohn calls "the three Cs" in his book *Punished by Rewards: The Trouble with Gold Stars, Incentive Plans, A's, Praise, and Other Bribes*) rather than command, control, and consequence, which are three Cs of a different color.

Having established that command and control is a short-term strategy limited by an unenlightened view of human responses and that the achievement of buy-in is the key to the long-term success and empowerment of human resources, we are left with three fundamentals that make it happen:

- *Shared values.* Buy-in occurs when everyone is on the same page in terms of values. If you're not sure—and if you aren't, this could be a pivotal time in your career—ask people to summarize their take on the values that empower success. Prioritize and share them with your team. Discuss issues that are in play and the way these values affect them. Identify behaviors and specific actions that support or detract from these values that exemplify or contradict them. Be open to the feedback that may come directly your way. Do this on a regular basis and you'll find your people holding one another—and you— accountable to a common set of values, all of which will lead to buy-in.

- *Project processes.* There is nothing dramatically surprising here other than this: When the inception of a project or mission (which can include challenging and imprecise issues such as culture and employee and customer satisfaction) occurs in a prosocial, non–command-and-control environment, buy-in occurs as a matter of process rather than as a desired state. All projects and missions require a clear understanding of *needs and benefits.* Then there is an *assessment of readiness*, which includes the analysis of resources, the identification of roles, and a means of measurement. There must be a congruency between the project and/or mission and the agreed-to values of the organization, with any gaps addressed and fixed. There also must be solid communication, feedback, and follow-through.

- *Shared decision making.* The simple truth here is that when people share the decision-making process (which, you should note, is not to say that they share in the decision itself), they are closer to buy-in. Always. Any time lost in a shared decision-making process is more than made up for during the implementation phase because all the inefficiencies born of a lack of buy-in are diminished. You are not looking for unanimous alignment here; instead, you are driving toward a *consensus.* The difference is that consensus allows for dissent, but in the face of a contrary majority, the dissenter ultimately aligns with the team in the name of buy-in. It's like a high-scoring guard traded to a team that has an even higher-scoring guard: The traded player has to accept a different role for the time being. This can happen only when all opinions and challenging aspects have been addressed, especially to the satisfaction of the dissenting party. Consensus management fosters not only buy-in but also creativity and innovation because people tend to flock to the dissenter to offer support in the name of team success. Trust is critical to the consensus-building process; dissent can never constitute a risk or carry consequences. All this requires the active participation and leadership of the manager, who is looking to guide the team toward a goal rather than dictating the goal.

Engineering the buy-in of your team isn't always easy, especially if the starting point is a command-and-control culture. However, if you stay the course and operate from a prosocial perspective, the tide will turn and soon you'll find that your troops are ready to march with you. The ultimate sign that you have achieved buy-in was perhaps best described by than Mahatma Gandhi, who said (paraphrased), "I must hurry, for I am their leader and there they go."

The idea isn't to get in front of them but to be *among* them.

In Chapter 5 we'll explore the power of storytelling and how it can help you establish your presence and influence others at a deeper level as you move them in the direction of your shared vision and objectives.

5

How to Master the Art of Storytelling for Personal and Professional Success

Why People Are Influenced by Stories

Good arguments and steely analysis are what make the business world go round. So say more than a few veterans of the executive suite, as do some of the MBAs who are launched into corporate internships straight from their graduate programs. Convinced that storytelling is something best done in a place that has a happy hour and among a few friends, they arm themselves with corporate jargon, expert terminology, and the latest version of PowerPoint with ever more bells, whistles, and graphics to dazzle the audience into submission.

However, from Harvard to Stanford and many places in between, the art and science of storytelling to achieve a business goal are wedging their way into mainstream business practices because a story can go where analysis is denied admission: the imagination. Cold hard facts can't inspire people to take part in a mission of change; straightforward analysis won't get people excited about a goal you're trying to accomplish unless you express it in a vision that fires the imagination and stirs the soul.

This is not new, of course; great leaders have always understood that the stories they tell are what make people launch themselves into battle for a greater cause and make the doldrums of daily life at the office or on the factory floor not just bearable but an important part of the journey toward the vision.

General Electric's Jack Welch understood this, as did Alexander the Great. Steve Jobs couldn't have accomplished what he did without a compelling vision, just as General Patton couldn't have conquered the Nazis without inspiring his exhausted and hungry troops to go on in the bloodiest days of World War II.

According to popular research, the appeal of storytelling can be traced back to the days when humans first started huddling together in groups, forming increasingly complex social orders that they could best track, make sense of, and pass on to others through the narrative. Evolution thus has made storytelling part of our DNA. To support this point, consider a study that was conducted during Patton's conquering crusade through occupied Europe.

In a 1944 experiment, the Smith College psychologists F. Heider and M. Simmel demonstrated people's tendency to make up characters and narratives from almost anything they see around them. Showing participants in their study an animation that included two triangles and a circle moving around a square, Heider and Simmel asked the observers what they saw. "The circle is chasing the triangles," people said, recounting the movements of the shapes as if they were part of a narrative with characters that had motives and intentions.

Subsequent studies have confirmed the human tendency to think and make sense of the world in terms of stories.

The filmmaker Robert McKee believes that storytelling is a critical component for anyone who's looking to build his or her executive presence. He alluded to it in this quote, which appeared in the *Harvard Business Review* in June 2003: "A big part of a CEO's job is to motivate people to reach certain goals. To do that, he or she must engage their emotions, and the key to their hearts is story."

More evidence that the way we think and what we believe are influenced by narrative comes from a 2007 study by Jennifer Edson Escalas, a marketing researcher at Vanderbilt University. She found that people had more positive reactions to advertisements that were presented in story form than to ads that were factually straightforward about the wares they were promoting.

The results of a different study, conducted a year earlier, undoubtedly give astute executives an idea or two about how to get their proposals accepted and their visions bought into by those they seek to influence. In that study, researchers found that when information is labeled as fact, it is subjected to critical analysis and the apparent human tendency to want to make it wrong, compared with information labeled as fiction, which people tend to accept more easily. Those looking to assert their executive presence as they strive to get a message across in a business setting therefore are encouraged to position their audience in story mode—as in "let me give you an example"—before presenting new ideas and to get listeners out of an analysis frame of mind that makes them itch to prove you wrong.

This explains why people often strongly associate actors—professional storytellers and characters that they are—with the roles those actors play on television. Stories circulate around Hollywood about how fans often are disappointed when an actor who plays a lawyer on the screen can't dispense legal advice or a TV doctor doesn't know why the rash a fan is having won't go away.

Putting It All in Context

In his book *Meatball Sundae*, the marketing guru Seth Godin writes: "People just aren't that good at remembering facts. When people do remember facts, it's almost always in context." The way to put facts into context for people is to transfer those facts through the use of a story because a story is all *context*, all the time.

Why is context so important for understanding? Why don't facts and naked data stick to the intellectual wall? Other than the fact that a story makes it more appealing, why wrap information into a story to help people remember it? For one thing, as we'll learn here, it's in our DNA. Storytelling is the oldest and most effective form of communication. From primitive cave drawings to men in robes standing on rocks before throngs of people, we have relied on storytelling to get our most important ideas across. Despite technology and evolution, the reasons it worked then are just as valid now.

Narrative magnetically—and, as you'll see later, biochemically—draws audiences into the process. It compels the listeners to visualize the narrative picture you're painting and helps them make connections. Stories show us who we are and who we want to be. When it's an organization you're talking about, who you are and what you want to be—to the customer, the community, and your team—reside at the top of the list of things you want the audience to understand. You don't want them only to hear and understand you; you want them to *feel* you. A recitation of facts and a roster of features are the slow road to getting that done, yet too often that is the default meeting agenda. A great story, in constrast, is a Ferrari on an open road leading to buy-in. As you're embracing storytelling to drive your executive presence, you'll want to make sure that you keep your eyes on the horizon to reach your goal of commanding respect the way the greatest CEOs do.

Learn to Structure and Tell Key Stories for a More Powerful Effect on Your Listeners

We come across many types of stories in our business and personal lives: in job interviews, investor pitches, hallway discussions, training sessions, private conversations, customer feedback boards, water cooler gossip, corporate meetings, and the evening news, to name a few examples. Below you'll find three key types of stories that you must know how to tell to teach, motivate, inspire, and manage so that you consistently create the desired perceptions and protect key reputations: yours and your brand's, which sometimes are one and the same.

Case Studies

This is the type of storytelling MBA students are peppered with ad nauseam during their studies, and for good reason, those at top business schools argue: Just as you can't become a seasoned pilot without spending considerable time in a flight simulator and later as the professional side-kick to the captain of a 650-ton A380 Airbus, you can't become a well-prepared captain of industry without first hearing and analyzing and then discussing your fair share of real-life business case studies.

Case studies are, of course, stories in an academic suit of clothes. Harvard Business School is famous for them, having the distinction of being the first business school to utilize case studies in MBA programs. Before that, formal case studies were in play primarily at law schools, where fledgling lawyers practiced their critical thinking skills on the stories their senior advocates had lived. Love them or hate them, outside of real blood-tears-and-sweat experience, case studies are often the closest a future senior executive comes to testing his or her mettle before succeeding at the front lines and in boardroom battles in the years to come. So what are case studies?

They are typically narratives in the form of written summaries of real-life business situations that are based on hard data and research. In studying these business narratives, students gain an understanding of the inner processes of an organization and what worked and what didn't in the pursuit of accomplishing the business's objectives over the course of time.

These case studies can describe anything from start-up funding issues to organizational change, innovation challenges, performance problems, executive succession issues, strategy decisions, and crisis communication, among the many scenarios that can arise within an organization. The list of possible topics is as varied and vast as the nuances of business and inherent situations.

Case studies offer plenty of flexibility for a business storyteller: They can be brief or highly detailed, personally experienced or the secondhand version of a classic real-life situation ripped from the financial headlines. Whether you were indoctrinated at Harvard Business School or received your education at a small liberal arts college in your hometown, understanding that your executive presence is strongly tied to your ability to craft case studies—or business stories—that explain, teach, inspire, and help solve problems for employees, peers, and bosses alike takes you another rung higher on the ladder to the top.

Developing a Case Study.   First, gather all the information and data you have about a particular case. Completeness of the information to be gathered is critical, as you want to make the case as close to the real-life situation as possible to deliver the most realistic learning tool for your audience. The data could come from formal 360-degree assessments, witness reports, performance reviews, and informal conversations with other stakeholders and direct customers, both internal and external, of the players. Similarly, formal questionnaires and interviews by an executive coach may provide deeper layers of insight into the situation.

As a second step, all the gathered data should to be structured in a logical way to accentuate the key issue of the case study. In the case of a dysfunctional relationship between an employee and a supervisor, for example, one that has communications issues and gaps at its heart, the data collected could be structured in sequential order to reveal how communication started off and then deteriorated between the two executives over the course of time within specific contexts, ultimately leading to an increasingly tense atmosphere in the work environment, missed opportunities, and an overall decline in morale and productivity.

The third step would be to make all these data highly digestible and interesting to an audience by creating a compelling narrative from the available facts. In other words, you create a story from data that people understand and relate to. Included in this narrative would be all the information that is necessary to understand the key issue, the players involved, the problems caused, and any measures that were taken to correct the situation. The narrative has to give the audience a complete picture of what happened, when it happened, who was involved, and where it happened. Your story may include personal information about two executives, their backgrounds, influencing relationships with others from bosses to peers, escalating factors such as stress, pressure from the C-level or customers, skill gaps, crucial conversations, early indicators of communication breakdowns and failures, and other known contributors to the issue. A well-told business story will help you assert your executive presence, but it can harm it if you lose sight of why you're telling the story, which is not for the story's sake. The case study is a critical learning tool, and its elements have to spark the audience's discussions, fuel deliberations, and arrive at different conclusions that can be tested, probed, and taken for a ride before the right decisions are made.

If the inherent negativity in many classic studies makes you want to renew your prescription for your favorite antidepressant, consider an additional benefit of these corporate downer stories.

The Teaching-Story: When Going Negative in a Case Study Can Improve the Results for Learners.   Although it makes sense that a story highlighting how people made good decisions and solve problems can teach an audience how to do the same thing, research says that when we're teaching through stories, we can increase the effectiveness of training by focusing on the errors and poor decision making that ultimately resulted in negative consequences. In a study cited in Robert Cialdini's book *Yes!* researchers used firefighters to test their hypothesis, finding that firefighters who experienced the mistake-riddled training scenarios not only paid more attention to the training and retained the information better but actually improved their judgment and displayed more adaptive thought processes than did those who got straight how to–based training.

The key to success is not only to show how things went wrong but to discuss what actions could have been taken to avoid the negative consequences. In other words, a type of reverse engineering of how things unfolded with the pros and cons mulled over, analyzed, and advocated or rejected by your peers can have tremendous benefits for the learners.

This sounds somewhat high-brow but is anything but that. Storytelling with a purpose is alive and well from the coal-dark mines of Pennsylvania, to the oil rigs of the North Sea, to the sand dunes of Iraq and the treacherous mountains of Afghanistan, and it's keeping miners, oil workers, and soldiers safe from harm in many cases.

An article in *Occupational Hazards* discusses the use of narrative in safety training: "Narrative—storytelling—can be an effective way to impart useful safety and health information to employees without insulting them or putting them to sleep." So says Elaine Cullen, Ph.D., CMSP, chief of health communication at the National Institute for Occupational Safety and Health's Spokane Research Laboratory. Dr. Cullen moonlights as an award-winning filmmaker in her spare time. She says this about storytelling in various blue-collar professions: "You learn by working with someone who knows how to do your job. You are an apprentice. You are mentored." She goes on to say, "When an experienced miner sees a new hire doing something really stupid, he often steps in and says, 'Let me tell you a story. I had a new hand do something like that before . . .' and he goes on to detail some negative consequence ranging from injury to death."

This type of cautionary and training-oriented storytelling can be transferred from the coal mines and the firehouse to Wall Street. Case in point: a fresh case study by Harvard Business School (HBS) that focuses on the collapse of the former Wall Street giant Bear Stearns.

In January 2009, the HBS professors Clayton Rose, Daniel Bergstresser, and David Lane published a case study, "The Tip of the Iceberg: JP Morgan and Bear Stearns," that analyzed what caused the financial juggernaut Bear Stearns to go down in flames and immortalize its officers in Wall Street history as reckless, inept, and hopelessly greedy. This type of study will keep first-year finance and corporate leadership MBA students on the edge of their seats as well as out of jail if the research is done right.

Success Stories

In contrast to the discussion-based learning delivered in negative case studies, the classic success story is designed to get people motivated, to spark an action that may lead to a better future, a desirable change, or an improved state of affairs. Although case studies and success stories are not mutually exclusive, the most crucial part of the success story, as its name implies, is an ending that results in, well, success. A happy ending is standard fare in thousands of Hollywood movies, and I suspect that that is partially responsible for the generally optimistic outlook on life among people in the United States compared with the Russians and the French, whose studies tend to be more pessimistic and whose movies focus less on a smiling protagonist at the end than on storylines that seem grittier and perhaps more realistically reminiscent of the hardships of life.

Why do we love happy endings? Neurological research tells us to thank the *reward center* in our brains for this. Upon perceiving a happy ending to a story, the limbic system releases a chemical substance called dopamine into the brain—the same stuff that makes us like sweets and a hot bath and all the other indulgences of life—and that gives us the kind of warm and fuzzy feeling that can lead to a state of euphoria. This often puts us into a frame of mind that is open to marching toward a brighter future with resolve and optimism.

A Fail-Safe Formula for Crafting a Success Story. Although you don't have to be Steven Spielberg, it helps manifest your executive presence if you have a formula that allows you to craft your own success stories that will do anything from making your audiences feel inspired and energized to mobilizing them to start on the path toward a better future as you lead the way.

The formula for a good success story starts with a *structure*. First, you want to introduce the characters in your story. The important thing here is that the audience can relate to the characters, recognizing some of the characteristics they share or recognizing the traits of others. In the movies, writers and directors cast with the hope that the audience will feel an emotional connection with the actors, either loving or hating the characters they play on the screen. The more the audience members relate, the more easily they'll suspend their disbelief and get pulled into the action.

Now that you've introduced the main character or characters in your story and made sure the audience relates to and cares about them, it's time for some dark clouds to move in. The essence of any story is conflict; the character has a need or a goal, and there must be an opposing force that stands in his or her way. In other words, you're describing a situation that clearly shows that it's not a good day at the client's office, the trading floor, the boardroom, or any other location people find themselves in when the proverbial trouble hits the fan. The audience members get the picture because they can relate: Trouble is brewing; a major conflict is threatening to shut down a vital project or ruin a critical relationship, and your protagonist is struggling to put out all kinds of metaphorical fires to keep the house from burning down.

Although the seemingly insurmountable obstacles your protagonists face may not include exploding bridges (unless you're an engineer) and high-speed car chases (unless you're a cop), all professions, from legal, to medical, to financial and political, can serve up their own horrific scenarios that can scare their key players to death and threaten their livelihoods.

Keep it realistic, though. You don't have the creative freedom that the makers of a multi-million-dollar movie enjoy. Also, your audience has to know or at least believe that the story you're telling is absolutely true; otherwise the desired effect of "this could be you" fades into the notion of "this would never happen in real life" among your eye-rolling audience.

Now it's time for a happy ending, one that comes about through the decisions and behaviors implemented by the protagonist: the very same things you are hoping the audience members will apply to their own situation through the story. Your hero has averted disaster, met a number of tough challenges, and saved the account.

It's worth repeating: The more the audience members recognize themselves and relate to the characters in a success story, the better. Similarly, the more closely the challenges that must be overcome match a situation your audience members are facing or are familiar with, the better the chances are that they'll be drawn emotionally into the tale. The happy ending will take care of the rest as dopamine floods the audience's collective brain and its mind's eye looks ahead as it imagines possibility and success just like the successful heroes of your story experienced.

Rumors

One of the most effective forms of storytelling and potentially one of the most damaging is the rumor. Rumors are created when only fragmented pieces of information are available and personal bias, motives, or fear fills in the gaps. Sometimes maliciously, sometimes innocently, whether sprouting from a kernel of truth or fabricated as twisted narratives of fiction, people tell stories that create certain perceptions in those who hear them, all too often with devastating consequences. From its power to cause irreparable injury to a reputation or financial loss measured in the multimillions, rumor is one form of storytelling that effective communicators need to know how to manage carefully and proactively.

On more than one recent occasion, rumors about the health of CEO Steve Jobs have taken a big bite out of Apple's earnings. When CNN's citizen journalism site iReport briefly mentioned that he'd had a heart attack, Apple's shares tumbled. Because of previous health concerns about Jobs—and the news having been reported by seemingly legitimate journalists—even Apple's quick response in labeling the news untrue didn't help. The stock was affected by rumor alone.

Rumors are almost impossible to trace, and that means it can be difficult to assign motive. The rumor about Jobs's alleged heart attack carried weight because it popped up on a CNN-branded site despite the fact that CNN did not create or confirm the rumor. With hundreds of millions having access to the Internet, chat room rumors and false breaking news are bound to continue to send shares rising and falling solely on the basis of mischief and the dark desire to cause havoc from the anonymity of a dimly lit den.

Obama and "Rumorgate." It's no secret that President Obama gained his initial foothold with the electorate through his prowess as a communicator. What is less known is that he, aided by a team of social media whiz kids, mastered the art of rumor control to keep the voting public's perceptions where he wanted them: close to the truth about him and his background.

An Internet audience monitoring firm called Hitwise reports that behind the scenes Obama's staff was quietly and strategically buying up specific search engine keywords and key phrases such as "Barack Obama" and other, more negative references to preempt unfavorable or untrue perceptions. It was a high-tech form of rumor management that directed people who searched for a certain key term to sponsored links that led to specifically designed—by Obama's people—landing pages in which the truth of pervasive rumors was clarified to suit the candidate's campaign. McCain's camp also purchased its share of key search terms, planting and combating the little nuggets of information called rumors that could mean a vote for or against the candidate. Never before had a presidential campaign been waged so vehemently in digital space, bringing new technologies and expertise to the front lines.

To create your executive presence and protect your reputation against unfair rumors, you could employ a similar strategy toward what is sure to become a staple in the strategy tool box of modern U.S. presidential campaigns.

Suppose you have a DUI citation in your past—a charge that was dropped—or got caught up in an ethics scandal—through no fault of your own—at a former employer. Perhaps a disgruntled former colleague or friend made disparaging remarks about you online that turned into rumors that could be accessed by anyone curious enough to search for you online. You could purchase the keywords that contain your name and refer to the rumor you would like to clarify and use them to lead searchers to a Web site or letter you post online that sets the record straight. Whether it's "John Smith DUI rumor" or "John Smith ACME Inc. Ethics Scandal," you want to make sure that upon searching for negative information based on a rumor about you, they get to your side of the story before seeing a legal or news report version that is less clear or is ambiguous. We'll talk more about managing your reputation online in Chapters 14 and 15.

To manage the perceptions of others and protect your executive presence from rumors, keep the following points in mind:

1. The more a rumor is repeated, the more people will believe it.
2. You need to respond to a rumor the moment it appears; otherwise it has time to spread virally through the Internet and reach the masses.
3. If the rumor is true, don't deny it. Confirm it and take control of the issue by framing it in your terms.
4. If the rumor is false, clarify the issue by pointing out the flawed premise directly. For instance, a rumor was circulating in one of my clients' firms that a supervisor who sometimes was perceived as unproductive and combative was reassigned to a different division of the company because management was afraid to fire him for fear that he would sue. The rumor was false, and the counterstrategy my client used to quash it was to tell the story that it would make no good business sense to burden another division of the company with an unproductive employee who wouldn't contribute value to the firm. He also pointed out the prior accomplishments of the employee and the specifics of his new role. The rumor was neutralized quickly because the staff had been given new and relevant information as opposed to filling in the gaps themselves in the incomplete story they had heard.

To debunk a false rumor, recruit credible third parties who confirm your story to the audience among which the rumor circulates. This could be within an organization or worldwide through the Internet and different media. For instance, if false rumors circulate among drivers that a certain make of car you manufacture has faulty steering columns, no amount of refutation you give can sway the public, but an all-clear endorsement from a competitor—good sportsmanship provided—or consumer protection group will eliminate motive and most likely silence the rumor mill.

Five Storytelling Techniques That Help You Convey Complex Ideas Easily and Persuasively

We frequently tune out. Our minds can't help wandering into more compelling territory when a presenter goes off on tangents or when structure and clarity are lacking and a clear point is light-years away. The following techniques will help you tell your stories with clarity, energy, a discernible theme, and appropriate emotion.

Technique 1: Pick a Theme for Your Story.

Great stories have a central theme that transcends the story: an insight to share, a lesson to be learned, a heroic deed to emulate, or a danger to avoid. Pick a single theme that will be crystal clear from the beginning to the end of the story and helps cement the point you are trying to make in your message.

Business and political themes can be:

- "David versus Goliath"
- "Phoenix Rising from the Ashes"
- "The Customer Is King"
- "The Leading Edge"
- "The Turning Point"
- "Thriving in Chaos"

- "They Said It Couldn't Be Done"
- "From Underdog to Top Dog"
- "It's Lonely at the Top"
- "Teamwork in Action"
- "Breaking New Ground"
- "Blazing the Trail"
- "The Comeback Kid"
- "Better Together"
- James Carville's famous "It's the Economy, Stupid," from Bill Clinton's first presidential campaign.

The options are endless. There are virtually no new themes for stories, just fresh interpretations of countless classic themes that have stood the test of time. If you have trouble coming up with your own theme, bestselling book titles can be a great source of themes you can borrow and base your story on.

Technique 2: Brevity Rules

"Be brief, be seated." The master orator Franklin D. Roosevelt said that one. Granted, he added "be sincere," but he knew that to get your message across, you have to respect the audience's time and, more important, its tendency to tune out if you go on for too long. And then, what would be the use of talking?

We live in an era of even shorter attention spans than in FDR's day, with faster and smaller bits of information competing for our attention, from BlackBerry texting, to 15-second TV commercials, to the mere 8 seconds of attention span that you have, according to research, to capture people's interest on your Web site before you lose them to a competitor. Keep this in mind when you tell a story: Tell only the most interesting and necessary parts and leave well enough alone. Once you make your point, move on.

Technique 3: Understatement Packs a Punch

Some trial lawyers are among the best storytellers in the world. The legendary Gerry Spence of Wyoming is one of them. Howard Nations, former president of the Texas Trial Lawyers Association, is another. In one of his publications, Nations tells the story of the late Moe Levine, a New York trial lawyer who used the technique of understatement in the summation of a case to such devastating effect that the result was the award of one of the largest verdicts in the history of the state of New York. Levine represented a man who had lost both arms in an accident. When the trial came to a close, everyone present, from the defendants to the judge to the counsel for the defense and the members of the jury, anticipated a long summation from Levine about the travails of a life with no arms. However, he surprised everyone. His concluding argument lasted no longer than a minute or two. It wasn't its brevity that won the day for his client. Its real power lay in the powerful understatement of what everyone knew yet no one thought about. Here's what he said, paraphrased by Mr. Levine, as reported by Howard Nations:

> *Your Honor, eminent counsel for defense, ladies and gentlemen of the jury: as you know, about an hour ago we broke for lunch. And I saw the bailiff came and took you all as a group to have lunch in the jury-room. And then I saw the defense attorney, Mr. Horowitz, and his client decided to go to lunch together. And the judge and the court clerk went to lunch. So, I turned to my client, Harold, and said why don't you and I go to lunch together, and we went across the street to that little restaurant and had lunch.*

He then took a significant pause before resuming:

> *Ladies and gentlemen, I just had lunch with my client. He has no arms. He eats like a dog! Thank you very much.*

You don't have to be a trial lawyer to create an emotional impact with understatement. Any time you want to emphasize a particularly strong point, you would do well to use the understatement technique instead of overexposing and thus weakening the drama of your story with long-winded verbiage. As in Moe Levine's closing at that trial, you can let the audience's imagination deliver the biggest punch.

Technique 4: Transport the Listener

You may not be Shakespeare, but you can try. Tell your story in the present tense. By doing that you will appeal to the unconscious mind of the audience, which research shows cannot differentiate between experienced reality and the emotions created by an event that is happening "right now" as you're describing it in your story. Think of all the emotional movie experiences you've had. You can get lost in the story because you are watching it unfold in the present, causing your emotions to respond to the action, making you feel anxious, sad, happy, or relieved. You can help your listeners live your story in the present by using active verbs, rich adjectives, and connotative words that stimulate the imagination. Interject suspense or surprise. Smile. Inject a little levity. Tap into the listeners' memories and thoughts. Change pace: Slow it down when there's a moment of drama and then speed it up to put them on the edge of their seats. Remember, people don't tend to remember facts unless they're presented in a specific context, and you have the power to control that through your storytelling.

Technique 5: Keep It Simple

Avoid the use of ten-dollar words. Instead of "It is not efficacious to indoctrinate a superannuated canine with innovative maneuvers," use the simple and time-tested "You can't teach an old dog new tricks." Simplicity and clarity work with any audience and are more appreciated the higher up the corporate ladder you go because top-level executives often see through attempts to mask a lack of knowledge or confidence with complex verbiage. Therefore, unless you don't care whether your message hits its target and simply aim to demonstrate to lower-level workers and civilians that you can speak at the C-level, jargon and words that aren't in most people's lexicon should be used sparingly. Keep this in mind: When listeners have a difficult time comprehending your message, they will not blame themselves for not getting it; they'll blame you. They'll reject the message and resent you for not being clear and concise. The following rhetorical tools will help you keep it simple.

Metaphor.   Metaphor is a straightforward, even poetic, way of describing a potentially complex concept in a compelling, easily understood way. Metaphors can help people vary their language and liven it up for the audience. They also function as verbal shortcuts to people's minds, quickly conveying an image or a meaning in just a few words. For instance, letting a colleague know that her comments during a meeting "added fuel to the fire" leaves little doubt about what is meant, informing her that she escalated a conflict rather than helped ease tensions without your having to go into detail. Similarly, telling your team that your biggest competitor is "breathing down your neck" indicates clearly that it's time to "buckle down" and "defend your territory."

Analogy.   An analogy is a comparison in which different items are evaluated point by point, typically with the intention of illustrating a point that's vague or not easily explained by referring to something that's instantly clear. Analogies are highly useful in providing insight into an issue as well as explaining more complex concepts. They're a type of extended metaphor. Former Secretary of State Henry Kissinger sent this memo in form of an analogy to President Nixon at the height of the Vietnam War in September 1969: "Withdrawal of U.S. troops will become like salted peanuts to the American public; the more U.S. troops come home, the more will be demanded." Here's a more lighthearted one from Robin Williams's character in the movie *Man of the Year*: "Remember this, ladies and gentlemen. It's an old phrase, basically anonymous. Politicians are a lot like diapers: You should change them frequently and for the same reason. Keep that in mind next time you vote."

Personification.   This is a technique that defines concepts or inanimate objects by referring to human qualities. John F. Kennedy, for instance, personified the word *country* in his inaugural address when he said: "Ask not what your country can do for you; ask what you can do for your country." More recently, Governor Bobby Jindal of Louisiana used personification compellingly in his victory speech after the campaign for governor: "Today, we begin a new chapter in the history of Louisiana. I've said throughout the campaign that there are two entities that have the most to fear from us winning this election. One is corruption, and the other is incompetence. If you happen to see either of them, let them know the party is over." The personification of the words *corruption* and *incompetence* made his message clear and personal.

True Change Doesn't Happen Overnight

Becoming a story-based culture that celebrates legendary tales of excellence, heroism, achievement, and action does not happen instantly or easily. It's an organic process that comes from within the organization through constant use of this technique on a daily basis. Like anything and everything associated with organizational culture, it begins at the top.

Storytelling is a cultural given whether the audience is told a story strategically or for social bonding and information-sharing reasons around the water cooler. Make this tool work for you, not against you. The power of storytelling has been with us since the dawn of time, and despite our reliance on all things digital—indeed, because of it—it will remain the heart and soul of the humanity of an organization. Your executive presence is strengthened by the stories you tell, and your storytelling may help propel your organization to new heights, new markets, and new opportunities.

In Chapter 6 you'll learn more strategies and techniques to influence people's attitudes and behaviors so that you can create mutual success and gain the respect you need as a leader.

6

Shortcuts to Influence:
The Secrets to Changing
Behaviors and Attitudes

WHETHER YOU ARE the CEO of a Fortune 500 company, the owner of a small business, or the manager of a small group of direct reports, there are few skills more critical than being able to influence others to change their attitudes and behaviors. For those doing the influencing, the stakes can't be higher.

For CEOs who have to sell change to their frontline employees — who need to adjust to changing market conditions, trends, customer preferences, and regulations and practices — to realize a vision, as well as start-up entrepreneurs who must influence bankers, venture capital firms, and business partners to adopt certain attitudes and behaviors that allow them to thrive and prosper instead of falling victim to the travails and missed opportunities and misguided decisions that lurk along the winding and obstacle-littered road to success, the ability to change attitudes and behaviors is anchored in the recognition of the difference between persuasion and manipulation.

Persuasion without Manipulation: Recognizing Attempts at Manipulation in Yourself and Others

From the moment we were born, we have been weaned and schooled in the art and science of manipulation, so much so that we hardly recognize it anymore both as targets and as purveyors of manipulative influence. It doesn't take a cynic to see that such ploys surround us at every turn, from a daily onslaught of advertising messages, to organizational politics, to a looming performance review. Our lives run on some combination of contingent consequence and tantalizing reward, with the latter often consisting of the avoidance of pain (obeying the law to sidestep a tax audit, for example). To escape this vicious circle of doomed cause and effect in the context of a manipulative management style—doomed because it inevitably leads to a downward spiral of disloyalty and mistrust—one needs to understand the difference between manipulation and the finer art of influence through ethical persuasion.

Manipulation is by definition a form of persuasion in that the avoidance of negative consequences serves the needs of the target audience. "You get to keep your job" is a tried and true example of a manipulative management strategy that is an effective enough response to anyone bothering to ask, "What's in it for me?" However, the key difference between manipulation and persuasion, one that differentiates successful cultures from fractured ones, is that manipulation is almost always a short-term strategy that is destined to self-destruct unless even stronger forms of manipulation are employed in the future. With manipulation, neither the manipulator nor the manipulated benefits over the long term. In the short term a manipulative strategy may yield the kinds of results that justify the means in the mind of the manipulator. If that's your modus operandi, consider changing it in favor of ethical influencing methods that build respect for you instead of corroding it.

Manipulation is all about getting people to do something for you rather than influencing them because there is something in it for them. The magic pill of the art of persuasion, conversely, is to get others to take action for themselves in a direction that serves the needs of the persuader as well, in other words, to devise a win-win proposition. Whereas manipulation is inwardly focused, persuasion is an outward connecting approach to exerting influence.

The fundamental element and criterion of effective and ethical persuasion is *trust*. Manipulators are heard, but persuaders are believed because they are trusted. Without trust, an audience hears on only one level: What are the consequences of compliance or apathy? With trust, audience members care about what they hear and give the message every chance to be meaningful on multiple levels: their own and the manager's. Trust is the mortar that builds teamwork, whereas manipulation is the jackhammer that tears it down. Manipulation is destined to expose itself as such and quickly breeds contempt when the reality of it kicks in. People who are manipulated try to find ways to survive, sometimes to get even, and those goals rarely align with the shared goals of the team. In the short term, manipulation may work, but for the wrong reasons: People are seeking an escape from negative consequences rather than feeling they are contributing to a unified goal. They react with fear rather than with passion. It's always preferable to persuade from within a win-win situation, an approach that will pay dividends long after the task or project window has passed.

Only through an understanding of the difference between influence through manipulation and influence through persuasion can we recognize it in our own experience on both the receiving and the dispensing ends of things.

There are several things to look for here:

- Is the incoming information (outgoing if you are the sender of the data) based on solid reasoning or on the fact that someone (perhaps you) is carrying a big metaphorical stick? Are emotions being appealed to, and is the specific emotion fear or positive anticipation?
- Are there alternatives on the table? To what degree is the recipient (perhaps you) being given latitude to choose a path, and is the path of least resistance the optimal choice in light of the consequences?
- What does the presenter gain from the logical choice? What does the other party gain? Who wins here, and at what cost?

- Do you trust the source of the information or choice being presented to you? If you are the sender, why should you be trusted as a source?

Once you make the shift from being someone who influences through manipulation to being someone who influences through persuasion, your leadership upside becomes unlimited. You'll never reach your potential alone, and in the end those who rely on manipulation often seem to find themselves in that position.

What Makes People Change Their Behaviors, Attitudes, and Beliefs?

The answer to this $64,000 question can unlock doors, win contracts, and sell ideas to the front lines and at the highest levels. Because attitude and behavior change is at the core of what any manager or leader does for a living, it pays to revisit a little Psychology 101.

We casually use terms such as *attitude* in daily conversations with others, often without realizing that a clear understanding of the word might help us understand others a little better. We say, "Lisa has the worst attitude today" or "This attitude isn't going to get you anywhere." A common question we hear or ask is, "What's with the attitude?" We give praise people directly and indirectly by saying, "Phil has shown a great attitude on this project." We use the word *attitude* in these contexts interchangeably with concepts such as mood, behavior, and demeanor. It helps to know that attitudes are more than just fleeting moods or a range of behaviors people display on a whim. Attitudes, as psychology defines them, are the positive or negative evaluations people make about other people, ideas, events, objects, and messages.

Test yourself for a moment: What do you think about the new customer management software your chief information officer introduced? Do you like your office door closed or do you prefer to work in an open environment where you can hear and see others around you? How do you feel about working overtime? What do you think about the new project you've been given to lead? What about the team members you're in charge of? What do you think about conservatives, about progressives?

Whether any of this pertains to you or not, you can see that you probably would have something to say about these or any other questions you could be asked.

To round out our understanding of what makes up an attitude, consider that attitudes can consist of up to three elements: cognitive (our thinking), emotional (how we feel about something), and behavioral (the actions we display).

Here's an example of a person's attitude that includes all three elements in the order listed above:

> *Paul believes that his lack of a postgraduate degree is holding him back in his career at his current company. He feels inferior whenever his M.B.A.- and Ph.D.-holding peers question his ideas and proposals. Whenever he can, he avoids presentations to this group and delegates the task to someone else.*

Before we can learn to influence or change a person's attitude and behavior, we need to know one more important aspect that pertains to attitudes: Attitudes have dimensions. Not all attitudes are equally strong, equally top of the mind, or strictly positive or negative. Here's an example:

> *Russell believes that outsourcing to offshore countries is bad for the U.S. economy and that it takes jobs away from Americans. Whenever he calls a customer service center and detects a foreign accent in the rep, he immediately feels anger, and his behavior toward that service rep shows it. Paul, like Russell, doesn't believe in outsourcing but understands why many manufacturers and service providers use lower-cost offshore companies for administrative tasks and customer service centers. In fact, his evaluations of the practice are ambivalent and equally negative and positive. When speaking to someone in India about upgrading his cable service, he barely notices the accent and doesn't feel strongly about it, and his behavior toward the service rep is not affected.*

The Science and Art of Changing Attitudes

To build your executive presence and command the respect needed to reach your goals, you must have the right attitude among your constituency. Whenever we need to accomplish an objective through others or get others to behave in a way that is in their own best interest, though it is not initially obvious to them, we can look to the social sciences to provide us with a several highly effective theories and principles to get us there.

Learning Theory

Leaders who understand learning principles such as classical conditioning, operant conditioning, and observational learning can use their knowledge to influence behavior and create win-win situations. Here's how to use the three principles to get ahead with people:

- *Classical conditioning*: Earlier we talked about the three elements an attitude can include: cognitive, emotional, and behavioral. If you employ the classic conditioning method, you can affect the way a person feels about something you're doing, selling, proposing, or encouraging and influence that person to form a positive attitude. For example, say you exchange a few friendly words with the receptionist every morning when you enter the office and always refer to her by name: "How was your weekend, Gina?" and "Do you have a busy day ahead of you, Gina?" and "Well, have a good day today, Gina." You elicit a positive emotional response from Gina and influence her to form a positive attitude about her job, the company, and you specifically. If everyone in the company does the same thing when he or she comes into the office, how do you think it will affect Gina's attitude throughout the day? Gina's pleasant attitude will make it possible to enlist her help with nontypical tasks when resources are tight and you need an extra hand. Gina will help you make copies without much resistance and without putting you on the proverbial back burner.

- *Operant conditioning*: Another powerful way to influence someone's attitude is by being aware of your response to that person's expressed attitude. Let's say Victoria asks you to give your input on a proposal she is preparing that she feels pretty good about. If you give her a positive response, you are reinforcing her attitude, making it stronger. If your response is negative—something like "I don't know, Vic; you're not really addressing the key concerns this client expressed in the meeting we had and the RFP we got in your writing"—Victoria's initial attitude inevitably will get weaker.
- *Observational learning*: Another highly effective way to influence other people's attitudes is to make sure they witness your reinforcement of someone else's attitude. Say you want more active participation in your morning meetings with the other managers in the firm. The more you reinforce people when they are expressing their feelings and giving input on the issues of the day, the more readily the less extroverted or vocal of the bunch will adopt the same attitude of participation because they are registering your reinforcement of the attitudes of those who take the initiative in joining the discussion.

Dissonance Theory

The social scientist Leon Festinger provided a gift to strategic persuaders everywhere when he introduced dissonance theory in 1957. Festinger's studies revealed that people tend to change their attitudes when they have attitudes that contradict one another. If they do not take action, the result of this internal conflict is *cognitive dissonance*, an unpleasant tension that people seek to reduce by dismissing any new information that would conflict with their original attitude or by embracing the new information and changing their attitude to be more consistent with their new worldview.

Here's an example of how persuaders can use cognitive dissonance to influence people's attitudes:

Using the earlier example involving outsourcing, we know that Russell has a strongly held attitude that outsourcing is not patriotic, eliminates domestic jobs, and hurts the economy. You are charged with cutting costs and increasing productivity. You introduce the idea to Russell, a key executive, that if you out-source certain tasks in the company to an offshore provider, the company can free up funds that will make it possible for Russell to hire another designer. That would make Russell's division more efficient, provide better service to clients, and ease the workload of the others, a constant source of stress that has led to conflict and hostility in the department.

Obviously, Russell can't help believing that an additional staff member would make his life easier and after envisioning this would feel a sense of relief that outsourcing might indeed affect his division in a positive way through less overtime, less tension, and quicker output.

Russell, who is experiencing cognitive dissonance between his original attitude of "outsourcing steals jobs" and his new attitude of "new staff would help our company on a number of levels and affect me personally in a positive way," has to make a choice: reject the idea or embrace it and change his original atti-tude so that he believes outsourcing can be an effective strategy in some cases. What he won't do is hold on to both attitudes because that would cause unpleasant tension that he would seek to reduce or eliminate.

Your job as the persuader is to tap into the values and attitudes in Russell that he subordinated or wasn't aware of until you introduced them as a possibility. By showing him the positive aspects (from his point of view) of a new attitude he could adopt and getting him to verbalize them, you've created cognitive dissonance and influenced a potential atti-tude change that results in a win-win situation for you and Russell.

Elaboration Likelihood Model

This model from the researchers Richard Petty and John Cacioppo posits that people change their attitudes and behaviors in more significant and lasting ways if they're exposed to persuasive messages that make them think and consider an issue in detail and depth. This is referred to as the central route to persuasion. It's important to note that people have to be motivated to hear your message, that is, find it relevant, as well as be able to process the message intellectually or physically. Distractions are a no-no if you want people to ruminate about something.

Persuasive messages that are lacking in substance but rich in peripheral cues such as the likability or the perceived authority of the persuader or any other associations that give the receiver a shortcut to accepting a message are thought to produce less stable and lasting changes in attitude or behavior, if any. That's called the peripheral route to persuasion. An example of this would be any number of 30-second commercials on TV that promise a better life via compelling images, music, and persuasive pitchmen and -women.

Successful executives can use both routes to persuasion by presenting reasoned, relevant, clearly communicated messages to their target audience, at the same time making use of peripheral persuasion such as authority, likability, and the ability to make others feel at ease.

Political candidates often are chosen by voters on the basis of peripheral cues that make decisions easier than wading through the issues and determining by thinking and elaboration which candidate may be more in line with one's personal goals and needs.

Let's go back to the idea of making others feel at ease because that's an element of exerting effective influence that is neither manipulative nor persuasive outside the context of the pitch itself. Let's call it the principle of *affinity*. People don't want to take orders from or be influenced by those who aren't cut from their own cloth or people they don't like. The more a manager can get on the same wavelength in terms of behavior and social standing (this is not meant to imply that managers should solicit loyalties born of friendship, which is a highly manipulative and risky approach), as evidenced by dress, use of language, and general demeanor, the better her chances are of influencing behaviors, attitudes, and beliefs. Nobody likes a manager who belongs to a country club one can't join. In other words, approaching others from their point of view and by using behavioral modeling rather than ignoring the inherent differences removes the obstacles of social distance and "strangeness." People respect one of their own who has risen to a position of authority faster and without close examination than they respect an outsider who suddenly comes into a position of influence and power.

An enlightened manager understands that the smaller the sociocultural gap is between his or her position and that of the direct reports being managed, the more effective his or her efforts will be in terms of exerting influence. If you are part of an organization in which a strict hierarchy determines the structure, work on breaking down the barriers as much as is feasible. Having lunch with the crew may be a place to start. When the president visits the troops at the front lines, he sits in the chow hall in their midst, eating the same food, shirtsleeves up, listening and responding to their stories.

Ten Powerful Principles You Can Use to Get What You Want without Violating Your Conscience

A leader's ability to influence others depends on the specific tools she has in her arsenal. Below you'll find a number of principles that will vastly and quickly increase your ability to persuade ethically. Although the principles are clear—old school manipulation is history; the empathetic win-win is in—the specifics of how to adopt and master a natural style of influence can be elusive without tactics that support the strategy. Here are 10 approaches that when combined and implemented will exceed the sum of their parts in making you a more persuasive rather than manipulative source of influence.

Approach 1: The Visibility Principle

Advertising professionals know that people gravitate toward the familiar. This is known as the *exposure effect,* in which familiarity breeds affection rather than contempt (that is perhaps more a domestic fact of life). This aligns with the concept of cultivating trust to become a better influencer: People trust what they know and understand and are skeptical of what they don't even if on the surface it appears to be positive. Enlightened persuaders get plenty of face time and interactivity with those they need to influence on a regular basis.

Approach 2: The Supply-Control Principle

There are situations in which using a limited supply of time or benefits can be a very compelling factor in terms of exerting influence. It's no accident that so many advertisements have a "limited time only" tag: We become urgent about that which is in limited supply. This is called the *law of scarcity*, and when it is used by enlightened communicators, it can translate into abundance in terms of a positive outcome. Be careful, though: By artificially limiting the supply of something others want and thus increasing demand, you are planting yourself on the manipulative side of persuasion. Creating demand by letting others know that what you're offering truly is in short supply keeps you in the ethical clear.

Approach 3: The Framing Principle

Words are powerful tools. They are so powerful that they become weapons of influence in the hands of professionals and reputation busters in the hands of the uninitiated. The reason words alone can influence people's thoughts and behaviors in a significant way has to do with what is called the *framing principle*, which refers to the creation of context and mental structures that evoke specific mental images and meanings that shape people's view of the world. If you tell someone to "disregard the gaps in my employment history" when applying for a job, rest assured that that's precisely what that person will be thinking about. The frame you evoked—"gaps in employment history"—raises a flag with the interviewer as her well-honed frame for that term may call up unfavorable concepts such as instability, restlessness, and lack of loyalty.

The negating of a frame actually creates the framework of the message itself, as one of our most famous politicians—a man known for his speaking ability, a true communications professional—discovered. In his first broadcast interview after his wife dropped out of the Democratic presidential race, former President Bill Clinton said he still had regrets and insisted he was "not a racist" despite controversies surrounding his comments about Senator Barack Obama's win in the South Carolina Democratic primary. More specifically, when the reporter asked, "Do you personally have any regrets about what you did while campaigning for your wife?" Clinton answered, "Yes, but not the ones you think. And it would be counterproductive for me to talk about." But then he did just that when he added, "There are things that I wish I'd urged her to do. Things I wish I'd said. Things I wish I hadn't said." As his coach, I would have advised him not to play into the reporter's hands by rambling on about any issues she didn't specifically address, as this can lead one into dangerous territory known as *streams of consciousness*. "But I am not a racist," he continued. "I've never made a racist comment, and I never attacked him personally." That single explosive comment was all over the news the same evening, with pundits from every network asking, "Who said anything about being a racist?" and "Where did *that* come from?" However, the fact that Clinton volunteered his thoughts without being pushed on the issue was only part of the problem, perhaps the smaller part.

The disclaimer Clinton issued during that interview could have come straight from the *Richard Nixon Book of Rhetorical Blunders*, a thick volume indeed. In Nixon's 1972 resignation speech, which was televised, he famously protested, "I am not a crook." For professionals with less media experience than these former U.S. presidents, there's much to learn here. According to recent research in the social sciences, disclaimers should be uttered with the utmost caution. Whenever a disclaimer is issued, such as "I don't mean to sound arrogant" or "I am not a racist" or any other comment that defines something you are not, the disclaimer directs attention to precisely the qualities you are disavowing.

Research shows that the unconscious mind cannot hear and does not process a negative sensibility; this means that the word *not* doesn't even register in the subconscious. This leaves the words "I *am* a racist" stuck in the mind. Although the conscious mind intellectually registers the word *not* in such a disclaimer, the unconscious mind, which records the entire experience on an emotional level, retains the memory of the word *racist*.

What does this mean for a savvy communicator? You never want to pin a negative label on yourself by disclaiming the very thing you are not.

Approach 4: The Authority Principle

People trust authority. Research has shown that people listen more carefully and trust more quickly when the information comes from a source they perceive as authoritative. Many people can recall meetings from early in their careers during which their contributions barely registered with others, whereas even the peripheral offerings of senior executives were accepted without question. Expertise from a credible source fosters trust. This implicit trust also transfers to authority that is merely perceived, often in just split seconds. To understand this, consider a well-known social experiment that illustrates the power of the common business suit, one of the many icons of authority. A young man in his thirties, impeccably dressed in a pinstriped suit, shirt, and matching tie, deliberately breaks the law as he crosses the street against the traffic light. The result: Almost four times as many people followed suit (no pun intended) as did so when the man wore a regular shirt and slacks in the same experiment. This is the *authority principle* in full glory, and informed communicators know that they can leverage whatever authority they bring to a situation to gain trust. As we've just learned, trust is the key to quick and effective influence.

Approach 5: The Evidence Principle

The *evidence principle* holds that information that is corroborated by outside parties—eyewitnesses, research, past experiences, and, best of all, the firsthand knowledge of the listener—is accepted immediately by the listener. This creates a framework of credibility and trust that a well-versed speaker can use to influence a listener more effectively. When an auto advertisement quotes an endorsement from *Car and Driver* magazine, for example, everything else the ad offers is imbued with credibility. The more uncertain the listener is about an issue, the more powerful the effect of such third-party confirmations and endorsements is, and the more credible the outside source is, the less trust depends on the nature of the information. The endorser is enough to win the trust of the listener, as in "If Warren Buffett thinks it's a good idea, that's where I'll put my money."

When using evidence in a presentation, take care to make it strategic and powerful. The nature of the way you use evidence depends on the situation. Sometimes you are trying to change an entire belief system, in which case the evidence you present is of paramount importance; at other times you are trying to reinforce someone's opinions and attitudes, in which case the evidence will support the appeal you make to the emotions. In either case, the use of evidence will get you to your goal faster and with lasting results.

Approach 6: The Likability Principle

As we've discussed at length, trust is a major factor in influence. It is the key that unlocks the door to moving forward. Without it, listeners will be wary and open only to manipulation, which is a short-term strategy that is bound to destroy trust and damage reputations in the long run. Trust is gained through a combination of factors. Likability is one of them. People more easily trust those they like. Likability ties in directly with similarity. We trust those who are similar to us. To influence others with likability, you have to express genuine interest in them. You have to speak their language by using words they use and frames of reference they understand. Making people feel comfortable by subtly mirroring their nonverbal communication contributes to the feeling of similarity.

Research shows that people base decisions on emotions before they check them against the facts. Trial lawyers have long known that the degree to which they and their clients are liked by jurors can make a difference in the final verdict. A study that supports this thesis was reported by Sanito and Arnold in *Trial Diplomacy Journal*. In that study, 600 jurors were interviewed after having reached their verdicts in a number of different cases. They were asked why they had decided as they had in reaching the verdicts. One key issue all 600 jurors reported as part of their choice of one verdict over another was "likability": the fact that they liked the lawyer in whose favor they decided each case better than they liked the other side's lawyer. The same rules apply to communicators who are not charged with influencing the perceptions of a jury. Be genuinely likable and focus on communicating the similarities you have with others to gain their trust ethically.

Approach 7: The Reciprocity Principle

We learned this one as children: If you scratch my back, I'll scratch yours. For adults it becomes the landscape of political lobbying, the fuel that powers relationships, as well as a powerful social influencing method. The essence of the *reciprocity principle* is concerned not as much with the trading of favors and things as with the exchange of value. Whether someone offers to baby-sit your children so that you can run an important errand, you offer to give someone a ride home from the office, or you refer a potential client to an acquaintance, a sense of obligation is established that dictates that something of similar value be exchanged at some point. The when, what, and how of the repayment vary with the context and the relationship.

If you choose to do a favor or provide value to someone first, you can trust that the action will be reciprocated at some point as the reciprocity principle triggers a strong sense of obligation in others. I'm not saying that you should do favors to get something in return, but by helping others when it is in your power and generally acting with generosity, you increase the potential for the types of relationships that make influence natural and easy.

Approach 8: The Experience Principle

This is the evidence principle taken to a personal level. Nothing says credibility quite like having been there, done that yourself. Confucius, a very enlightened communicator, said: "I hear and I know. I see and I believe. I do and I understand." This is something we, as influencers, can take to the bank.

We experience life in multiple ways, all of them sensory. A knowledgeable communicator knows how to bring this sensory, experiential realm into presentations in a manner that adds credibility and trust within the context of the intention of the exchange. The more you can help your constituents have a visceral experience either directly or indirectly through the stories you tell, the more you will reach them at an emotional level and the more you will be able to influence them. Keep this in mind when you have to engage others with a story. Since they won't experience the reality of the story, it is up to you to create the perception of reality.

Approach 9: The Highlighter Principle

When we're trying to get a message across and influence others, we naturally tend to focus on what supports our argument and play down what might be contrary to it. We all do this. Politicians, spouses, ministers, the media, and managers do it every day in the course of trying to influence others. The issue isn't that such slanting is right or wrong but is a matter of what's fair or biased, what's responsible or manipulative, and, more aptly here, what works to build credibility and establish trust when you influence and what doesn't.

We should amplify elements of information that conform to all the other principles presented here: those which build trust, those which create a win-win, and those which don't take advantage of others for one's own gain. As we highlight the information we consider important to our message, we have to be careful not to omit information that speaks to the needs, values, and goals of the audience. Although it can be difficult and counterintuitive to bring up information that's contrary to the message we're trying to get across, ethical persuaders present both sides of an argument and show the validity and benefit of accepting their side.

When we exaggerate the truth—or turn up the volume on what we want the audience to believe—in a way that hides or alters the facts of any counterpoint, we're closer to manipulation than to a higher and longer-lasting form of persuasion. Strive to present a full and fair argument, using evidence and experience and all the other methods to influence. You can highlight, you can focus, but you can't exclude any portion of the truth without being manipulative.

Approach 10: The Passion Principle

Passion can't be explained. It is felt. Whenever you are looking to influence someone to accept your ideas and share your vision, you have to have a feeling that energizes your insides, that makes you become expressive and use language that stimulates the heart as well as the mind. If it doesn't come easily, think about it and focus your thoughts on the aspects of the idea that you can feel in your gut. Then amplify that feeling and share your message.

In Chapter 7 we'll look at the issue of interpersonal conflict and how we can manage relationships effectively to reduce negativity and build lasting rapport in our quest to create an executive presence that commands the respect of those around us.

7

Secrets to Managing Interpersonal Conflict and Improving Relationships

---

IF YOU'VE SPENT more than a day or two wandering the halls or filling a cubicle in a corporation or another type of organization—including schools and federally funded bureaucracies—you know that death and taxes do not have a monopoly on inevitability. In fact, even if the head count of your organization amounts to only single digits, you probably have the scars to prove it. Anywhere two or more people occupy the same space, professional or otherwise, in the context of a shared mission and under the looming shadow of personal goals, the laws of human behavioral dynamics kick in. When they do, sooner or later the inevitable result is conflict.

Anyone aiming for a top-level spot on the organizational flowchart as an executive knows that no matter what the culture is or how evolved the people who constitute it are, conflict is going to happen. It's like weather is to pilots and blood is to surgeons: At the end of the day success depends not on its avoidance (which is *not* going to happen) but on how well you land the airplane or sew up the patient. In other, more direct words, the issue—and the inherent opportunity—with interpersonal conflict is a process that is much more enlightened than conflict *avoid-ance:* the *optimization of consequences* when conflict does arise.

Conflict in a dynamic business environment is an experience that people almost always analyze in retrospect rather than in the moment. The business school case studies we discussed in Chapter 5 are a classic example of the documentation of conflict and our attempts to learn from the experiences of others who occupied the corner office — or office cubi-cle — before us. Looking back, it's often easy to see that the dynamics of interpersonal conflict within teams and among colleagues usually have two distinct elements (not to mention two or more sides of the story, which is not the point here):

1. Concern for the *outcome* (who wins, who loses, and what it all means), regardless of how those chips happen to fall
2. Concern for the health and nature of the ongoing *relationship* between the participants

The latter is a can of worms influenced by organizational hierarchy and history. Healing a riff with your boss is very different from patching things up with the fellow in the next cubicle, but unless you wear a hel-met and carry a weapon to work every day, this is an organizational factor that has to be managed.

Common Causes of Interpersonal Conflict

Most people don't require a definition of conflict any more than they need to know what Webster says about hunger. However, in this case a definition can be helpful because conflict too often is written off as one party making another party angry by not giving the second party his or her way or by being obnoxious and unreasonable. Although this is a plau-sible definition, a better one is this: Conflict is a dynamic that occurs when one person does not receive the expected or desired response or behavior from another person.

This is, of course, a very expansive landscape of potential dust-ups. For rising executives whose organizational success depends on the support of various teams and other corporate stakeholders, the matrix of variables here is deep and wide, resulting in a nearly infinite combination of combustible dynamics that meet the definition without compromise: everything from personal values, to preferences and needs, to resentments and triangulated agendas. When conflict emerges from the frequent interactions of colleagues and peers or bosses and direct reports, it's sometimes less an issue of who is right and who is wrong and more a matter of a *stylistic* difference: a clash of perspectives seasoned with a dash of insensitivity. In a conflict, a tiny speck of emotion can detonate an otherwise reasonable disagreement.

In his 1992 book *The Eight Essential Steps to Conflict Resolution* (it should be noted here that we'll be offering executives who are looking to build a powerful presence 10 new ones later in this chapter), Dr. Dudley Weeks presents the following seven categories of causal factors that can result in an interpersonal conflict:

Differing Worldviews and Cultures

Don't look now, but not everybody thinks the same way you do. Although you may be tolerant and understanding, that doesn't mean other people view you that way. It may be a fundamental difference of opinion, but it also may be that they aren't coming from the same place, that the parties to the dispute view the world through vastly different lenses. Some corporate cultures honor the elderly; others push them into the background. Some place male and female workers on different levels. Your company may be taking the high road, but if you or your supervisor brings a contradictory cultural perspective to work, one that isn't in synch with those of others, the potential for interpersonal conflict is high.

Priorities

You need money; someone else needs recognition. You need respect; someone else needs, well, money. You need order; someone else thrives on chaos. In a department with eight people, you are likely to find eight different sets of needs, each of which is a potential bomb when it collides with the conflicting needs of others.

Perception and Filters

You may think you're a funny person; someone else may find your sense of humor caustic and mean. Similarly, what you find important and urgent may be perceived by others as residing farther down the list of priorities. You may be perceived as unfriendly when you feel you're simply serious about the work at hand. Such misperceptions can lead to conflicts during which these differences in perception tend to exacerbate the problem and warp the real issues.

Power

Some people have it and like to use it to get their way just for the sake of getting their way. They *must* win. Without a rationale, this usually results in some form of conflict because people resent being manipulated and in essence being pushed around. Other people may resent those with power they don't have and take steps to undermine them so that they can feel more equal.

Values and Principles

It's a free country, but that doesn't mean that all the people in an organization are free to do what they believe is right or, more troublesome, what they please. You may want to take the day off on a certain holiday because of your beliefs, but your company—and your boss—may not allow it. This easily can result in conflict, and if you press the point by doing what you think is right and what you want to do, it also can result in conflict.

Feelings and Emotions

There's honesty, and then there's brutal honesty. Two coworkers may have vastly different thresholds for what constitutes directness and clarity versus harshness and bullying. Emotions can be the enemy of productive conflict resolution even though they may be the causal factor. In this case, the faster they are removed from the discussion, the more efficient the resolution process is.

Internal Conflicts

This catchall could pertain to people who bring problems at home to work with them as well as personality conflicts, substance abuse issues, hidden resentments, and a host of other issues that when not successfully managed easily can lead to conflict with another employee. Regardless of the source of the conflict, there are always stakes surrounding a successful resolution. Once upwardly mobile managers and executives learn to recognize these originating sources as potential conflicts in the making, they can prepare for and minimize what seems to be an inevitable conflict.

How to Recognize and Prepare for Brewing Conflicts

The way people recognize and deal with emerging conflicts is a reflection of many variables, including their experience. The fact is that what bothers one employee may not bother another in the slightest, usually because of the life that employee has led and the lessons he or she has learned from it. Add to this the fact that conflict resolution is a skill completely separate from friendliness, openness, and sense of humor, and we face a complex challenge when we attempt to generalize a response.

The warning signs of impending interpersonal conflict in the workplace differ from person to person. Clearly perceivable yellow flags may be noticed, or, at the other end of the spectrum, someone who seems perfectly happy one day may go off the deep end, up to and including the dark incidents one occasionally hears about on the evening news. Rather than generalize behaviors, it is better to look for behavioral and attitudinal *variance* in the people with whom one works. Someone who for years has been friendly and jovial but lately seems down and quiet may be a source of conflict in waiting. Changing patterns of attendance and tardiness can signal trouble, as can unexpected requests for time off or changes in schedule or assignment, especially when motivated by a desire to get away from someone else.

Although it's risky to assume that any of these symptoms is signaling that an employee is ready to detonate, it's prudent to look closely and see if there's something you can do to help; incidentally, this provides a bona fide opportunity to assert your executive presence in the context of the situation. The employee may be timid about coming forward with personal issues that are manifesting in his workplace behavior and even more hesitant to tell his manager about an issue he is having with a fellow employee or with the company. Yet if you notice a difference in an employee's attitudes and behaviors and can intervene in a positive and helpful manner—versus a disciplinary or arbitrating one, which is often the case after conflict has surfaced—you stand a chance to minimize whatever potential conflict resides just below the surface. In addition, the respect you'll probably gain from the interaction—or intervention— contributes directly to others' perception of your executive poise.

Preparation for conflict resolution comes in two flavors: creating a means of *prevention* and offering resources for *resolution*. The former includes having an employee grievance process in place as well as a safe way to discuss issues with supervisors or coworkers in a confidential manner. Some companies offer counseling to employees whose problems warrant that level of attention, and others train supervisors in spotting conflict before it happens and intervening accordingly. If neither measure applies to your work environment, you can assert your status as a rising executive and approach appropriate stakeholders in the company— human relations might be a good place to start—to discuss the possible adoption of an effective conflict prevention and resolution program. This is not a bad initiative to have on your curriculum vitae when the time comes to ascend the corporate ladder another rung.

Back in the trenches, once a conflict has ignited, the response becomes trickier, especially when the supervisor or leading manager is part of the square-off. Firm company policies can mitigate the problem here, such as a no-physical-contact rule whose violation can result in immediate termination, a take-it-behind-closed-doors rule, the availability of immediate mediation, and a culture of peer involvement and enforcement to help employees resolve issues quickly among themselves. The rules and boundaries of behavior during conflict, especially those which are culturally accepted, create the optimal environment for resolution when the need occurs.

Conflict is not inherently a bad thing. If everyone agrees about everything all the time or if management never is challenged because of fear of reprisal—in other words, if employees have no voice—by definition a cultural ceiling has been placed on the company's potential. For business professionals on their way up, it's critical to embrace the idea that what causes a conflict is less important than the means and consequences of resolution. In enlightened organizations this becomes an opportunity for growth and cultural vitality, not to mention the chance for aspiring leaders to build their executive presence by practicing the principles you're about to learn.

Good Conflict versus Bad Conflict

The manifestation of conflict can be viewed as an opportunity to strengthen relationships and fortify cultures, though this can happen only when the ground rules and consequences line up with a process of healthy debate. Without such rules of order and in the presence of unfortunate consequences, relationships and cultures almost always take a hit when trouble arises.

In marriages and long-term relationships, for example, conflict is as opportune as it is inevitable. It presents a chance for the partners to clarify intentions, perceptions, and feelings, to be heard and to hear. A committed relationship grows through conflict, or at least it should. In a perfect world, the result is an opportunity to make changes as part of the resolution process, to strengthen respect and solidify the process of healthy communication. This model works just as well in an organizational culture, corporate and otherwise, where a wider range of personal issues and styles is more acceptable than it may be in a marriage. When the model is executed poorly, in either environment, the result is likely to be resentment, anger, and an ongoing agenda of revenge that is never healthy for the relationship and begins a vicious circle of conflict.

One principle applies to the healthy resolution of conflict in a marriage, on a ball field, or in the workplace: The result must be, at least to some degree, a win-win proposition. Aspiring executives working to strengthen their poise and presence understand that there can be no clear-cut losers and no punishment for honestly and productively engaging in a disagreement that takes place within acceptable boundaries. Both sides of a conflict must understand and accept this principle because when they do, the intention is, by definition, to move forward rather than assign blame. Most of the time one side walks away with a bigger "win" than the other—this is another way of saying that one party usually compromises more than the other does—but even so, it means that understanding, empathy, and some measure of give-and-take has been integral to the resolution process. Healthy conflict resolution brings all parties to the negotiation table with the intention not so much of winning but of achieving a win-win solution. There is such a thing as being dead right, which means that even though your argument emerges as the unquestioned winner, the cost—in terms of relationships, reputation, respect, and harm to your executive presence—may exceed the benefit.

Most people, at least those with some command of their emotions, engage in conflict with some sort of *strategy* in play. It may simply be their default style, such as withdrawing into a silence imbued with the promise of getting even later, or it may be totally calculated. This style of withdrawal is common when one party doesn't view the stakes as having as much weight as the other does, allowing the first party to give in or simply disregard the opposing argument. This is far less than a win-win resolution and can lead to resentment and disconnection, with a high likelihood that further conflict is right around the corner.

Some conflicts are the exact opposite; they resemble a full frontal attack. This happens when one party views the outcome as more important than the relationship, a sort of "get out of my way or I'll run over you" approach. Managers have been known to adopt this strategy—it's called old school management—almost always at a cost to morale, respect, and their standing as a poised and respected executive.

Many people are natural conflict *avoiders*. Facing conflict is their final option, one to be avoided at all costs, and in avoiding it they bottle up frustrations and resentments, perhaps even skewing the truth by minimizing or compartmentalizing their arguments to save face. These people value the relationship above the consequences of resolution (an unappreciated or bullied and disgruntled coworker is an example right up to the

moment an unexpected resolution with a frightening emotional outburst—or even a shotgun—surprises everyone), and this does little to
move toward effective resolution by addressing the issues at hand directly.

A strategy that can work both ways is *compromise.* This occurs when
in the name of achieving a win-win outcome, one party gives up something she originally wanted while retaining an alternative or partial gain.
The compromiser believes that mutual satisfaction is not only possible
but preferable to continued conflict and is willing to accept the resolution
without further resentment. The problem here is that when this doesn't
happen, when a compromise is accepted and later resented, the result is
an assurance of further conflict.

Perhaps the most productive strategy for conflict resolution is *direct
confrontation.* However, this works only when both parties engage within
the context of striving for a win-win and place a high value on the relationship as well as the resolution of differences. In the workplace, this
takes the form of moderated debate and coworkers who have been
trained in productive ways to confront one another. In other words, there
are *boundaries* in place when it comes to resolving differences. Without a
mutual desire for a win-win outcome, confrontation boils down to who
has the bigger hammer—the supervisor who has the last word or the party
with the most logic behind his or her case—in a culture that has no
boundaries or mechanisms for making sure such conflicts conclude satisfactorily. For business professionals who are looking to make a positive
impact in their organizations, building and reinforcing their executive
presence in the process, conflict provides a great opportunity to test their
mettle and show enlightened leadership. The following section offers
tools and strategies to aid in that process.

Ten Powerful Ways to Resolve Conflict, Restore Harmony, and Strengthen Interpersonal Rapport

Although conflict should not be and rarely is a recreational pastime or a
game, it's easy to compare the skills it requires to those used by successful
athletes. Athletes train endlessly for specific situations, but in the heat of
a competitive battle they must resort to instinct and muscle memory,

bolstered by the strength and conditioning they've achieved in noncompetitive workouts. On the field of battle there isn't always time to think and strategize; you need to *react*, to make your move, to seize opportunities and optimize your movements.

The same thing is true of interpersonal conflict resolution: You can read all the books and practice all the role-played guidelines, but when emotions are high and your opponent doesn't seem to be as concerned as you are with the win-win, when he or she is calling you out or threatening your reputation, honor, or standing, it can be challenging to keep your cool. Athletes have muscle memory and a trainer to help them prepare, but managers and professionals striving to bolster their executive presence can and should adopt the following techniques to their conflict resolution repartee not so much to win as to navigate conflict situations toward outcomes that include strengthened relationships, a greater sense of teamwork, and a mutual resolve to take the organization forward.

1. *Use active listening.* We've had coaching that instructs us to "be in the moment." With conflict resolution, this means listening carefully to both sides without an emotional filter the way a judge listens to lawyers pitching their cases. If you're a manager arbitrating a conflict between two employees, this is easier than it is if you're a party to the conflict. Nonetheless, hearing and understanding the logic and reasoning of both sides is critical to the creation of a mutually satisfying resolution. The term *listening* in this context applies to more than words; you should strive to perceive messages through facial expressions and body language, which can speak volumes.

2. *Separate the positions from the issues.* Too often in the heat of conflict, the difference between a position and an issue can be lost. An example here would be negotiating for time off. The issue may be company policy and fairness, and the position may be the requesting employee having worked significant uncompensated overtime. Focusing on one without a contextual consideration of the other creates a bias that can be harmful to the creation of a mutually satisfying solution. Begin with the issue and then view the positions in that context.

3. *Understand and validate.* As an arbitrating manager, it is critical that you not only seek to understand both positions in a conflict but also *validate* each party's claim to what he or she believes is right. This doesn't mean that you agree, only that you can see that party's point. This alone opens the parties to compromise or an outcome that doesn't go their way. People often want respect and consideration just as much as they want to get their way. In the game of win-win, sometimes emerging emotionally intact is enough.

4. *Empathize.* The power of empathy in conflict resolution cannot be overstated. Empathy happens when you put yourself, minus your biases and personal experiences, into the shoes (the circumstances) of both parties or, if you're one of the combatants, into those of your opponent. Try to see it from the other person's point of view and you may find that the picture takes on a slightly different hue.

5. *Implement boundaries and expectations.* Because you are a manager, people are looking to you to clarify boundaries and expectations for behavior and outcomes. If these things are muddy in the middle of a conflict, your job is to clarify them for both parties. The idea here isn't to reprimand but to prevent emotion from clouding the boundaries of behavior and expectations for roles, behaviors, and outcomes. A good way to open this can of behavioral worms is to ask both parties to state what they believe are the boundaries and expectations that pertain to the issue at hand, using their perspectives as a platform for your clarification and reinforcement. This approach breeds open and honest communication and will keep both parties within acceptable boundaries as you work through the issues.

6. *Be tactful.* This may not be easy, as one party or both parties may be way out of line from the outset. Don't get sucked into the emotion of the issue and don't convey even the slightest sense of disrespect for the parties or their views even if they originated on another planet. If you remain sensitive to their feelings, they'll remain open to your input.

7. *Explore the issues and alternatives.* The parties to a conflict rarely are interested, at least at first, in looking at things differently. It's your job as the arbitrating manager to help them do this, and it happens when you begin exploring alternative views and solutions with them. Ask open-ended questions such as "How would you act differently if this policy were reversed?" that require thought and elaboration. If you can get them to talk about an alternative, you're on the way to getting them to accept one.

8. *Use "I" statements.* When you are a party to a conflict, using a first-person context is much more productive than making statements that easily are perceived as wrong. If you say, for example, "I was angry when you said that about me," you'll be greeted with more openness than you would be if you said, "What you said about me was wrong." People can't argue with how you felt, but they can certainly dispute the right or wrong of things. Keeping it centered on how you feel avoids accusation, which, when it happens, is like throwing fuel on the fire of conflict. When you take responsibility for your actions, especially when they bump up against the boundaries of acceptable behavior, the opposing party will be more likely to do the same thing.

9. *The power of stroking.* It may sound manipulative, but if you can find something positive to say about the other person in the heat of a dispute, that person will be more open to hearing what you have to say about the issue at hand. Stroking the other person says you aren't attacking her character and haven't lost respect for her, only that in this instance you disagree with something that was said or done. Conflict goes off the rails when it becomes personal, and ironically, injecting something personal in a positive manner is the best way to keep it from going there.

10. *Attack the issues, not the person.* Conflicts sometimes are smoke from another fire, or the surfacing of past disagreements or personality conflicts. When you sense triangulation entering the argument—the use of an unrelated opinion or issue to

create a negative context for the present one, such as "You always put yourself first in these situations"— you know that this is personal rather than issue-driven. As an arbitrating manager, listen for anything that is personal in nature and bring the conversation back to the issue as quickly as possible.

How to Nurse a Strained Relationship Back to Health

Emotions are real and powerful factors in people's behavior and relationships. Like any other aspect of life, they need time to heal when they are injured.

The key to healing a broken or strained relationship is to let go of the emotions that remain after the issue has been resolved. Holding a grudge won't add luster to your executive presence or foster respect from peers, colleagues, and higher-ranking executives. Although resentment is normal, it is also destructive. If you owe someone an apology, give it. If someone owes you an apology, make it easy for him by extending an olive branch first, showing that you harbor no hard feelings and forgive him (this is better shown than told). If you have trouble forgiving and letting go of resentment or negative opinion, seek counsel from a trusted coworker or even a professional if you feel it is compromising your work or experience.

Usually, after the smoke has cleared, you'll see things differently from the way you did when you were stoking the fire of the conflict. Take a close look at the realities that define the nature of the post-conflict relationship: Does the other person harbor resentment or jealousy? Are there things in her life or yours that have a bearing on the relationship even though they remain below the surface? Is the other party simply having a bad day that has nothing to do with you? Sometimes you have to earn your way back into the heart and mind of someone with whom you've had a conflict, and the best way to do it is to be friendly and show interest in his feelings, his opinions, and his work, to be available rather than distant. This evolved and proactive approach will add important dimensions to others' perception of your executive presence and poise.

It may not be all about you. Try to notice how the person relates to other people, what her attitudes and behaviors are in general rather than specifically toward you. Then ask yourself how tolerant you are or even how paranoid you are toward this person when in fact her attitude and behavior may not relate to you or the conflict in any way. When that's the conclusion, it's easy to let go of harbored resentment and cut the other person some slack.

One of the most powerful ways to heal a strained relationship is to go right at the problem. Invite the other person to coffee or even lunch and lay it on the line, not with the intention of revisiting the conflict but to mend the relationship. Besides restoring harmony, this has the critical value of showing executive poise. As part of the process, establish a new set of rules that are centered on open and honest communication in a context that honors your respective roles as teammates and coworkers. This is the time to make things personal, but only insofar as your relationship is affecting the workplace and your satisfaction within it. People appreciate honest feedback that is void of judgment and negative emotion, and when the intention is to heal and move forward rather than revisit the past, you'll find the process easier than you expected it to be. When it comes to forgiveness, ask and most often ye shall receive.

In Chapter 8 we'll look at how we can assert and reinforce executive presence and gain respect by managing difficult conversations: the conversations we'd rather not have but need to have in various situations for personal and professional success.

8

How to Hold Conversations Nobody Wants to Have

A STRONG EXECUTIVE presence is an asset when you're a counterparty to a difficult conversation. The confidence and professional poise you exude can imbue the situation with a healthy sense of respect. Also, successfully negotiating a difficult conversation can add another dimension to your stature as an influential executive presence. Incidentally, a corporation is a unique and challenging place to have a difficult conversation. The same is true for any type of organization in which a hierarchy is in place, especially when careers and paychecks depend on some semblance of order and responsibility. Difficult conversations are usually easier in, say, the military or at the local police station, where someone with enough stripes on her sleeve can summon someone without rank and without fear of social consequences and tell that person that he screwed up or is being assigned to a location without plumbing. Being held accountable, being coached, being corrected, and being on the receiving end of bad news are part of the organizational experience for managers and foot soldiers alike. Because these things are delivered by human beings—not all of whom are enlightened in the art of commanding respect like a CEO—such conversations occur with wide variations in effectiveness and empathy.

We've all been on the receiving end of difficult conversations. We've been challenged, reprimanded, reassigned, realigned, and, in some cases, fired. We've been called on the carpet, summoned to the boardroom, and put out to pasture. Unless it was done with some measure of tact and skill, chances are that we remember the conversation with a distinct lack of fondness. On the other side of the table, most managers have faced the prospect of delivering feedback, discipline, and even the proverbial pink slip and have found the process just as stressful. However, as with most managerial skills, there is a learning curve that can help aspiring leaders establish the critical perceptions that set them apart from their peers.

The process of having difficult conversations—whether incoming or something you originate—can be made more effective and less stressful through an understanding of certain principles and the adoption of certain behaviors that minimize defensiveness and open the listener to the feedback, which is an essential factor in the creation of meaningful change. In the process, you're creating the kinds of perceptions that help you build a powerful executive presence and command the respect of your peers, colleagues, and bosses.

The Anatomy of a Difficult Conversation

Difficult conversations are rarely simple. They may seem straightforward, but below the surface there is an entire textbook of human psychology suddenly kicking into overdrive. They are almost always a manifestation of introspection and response on several levels simultaneously and from both parties. When one of those levels is left untended, the outcome of the conversation, at least in terms of the way the feedback or bad news will be received, is less certain. To complicate matters, it's more common than not that the prospect of having a challenging conversation puts the delivering party in a difficult position. As ambitious business professionals aiming for a top spot on the organizational chart, we may know our way around a spreadsheet, but the idea of tackling a tough conversation with a long-term employee places us in a position of anxiety and hesitancy. Those two approaches — *anxiety* and *hesitancy* — are often the very things that compromise the intended objective of the conversation in the first place.

Although the conversation may seem focused, from a psychological perspective there are actually three conversations — or, if you prefer, three levels of conversation — taking place at once:

1. *The "what happened" conversation*. Although this is the surface conversation and consists of the actual words that are used, it isn't quite that simple: It also includes nonverbal communication, the stuff that adds nuance and emphasis in a way that words cannot, including the implications of the unspoken (substantive facts and elements that are left out of the narrative). A boss who sits with an employee and leans forward while speaking softly and with obvious empathy delivers a message far different from the one delivered by a boss who stands over a subordinate with arms crossed while speaking with a raised voice and staccato delivery. The sum of form and function may constitute the intended message, but the verbal message is only one of three elements that must be managed to optimize the opportunity. Each party to the conversation often enters the exchange believing he or she is right, and that belief necessitates management of the other two levels.

2. *The "feelings" conversation*. In the real world the term *difficult* is synonymous with *emotional*. Emotions occur on both sides. The deliverer of feedback experiences anxiety, which often is compensated for by insensitivity masquerading as directness. The receiver experiences hurt feelings, wounded pride, and defensiveness. More often than not, both parties try to hide their true emotions, and that in itself becomes a variable in the conversation that if not managed can get in the way of clarity and effectiveness. This may be contrary to human nature, but the most effective means of preventing this is to be open about how the conversation is making you feel rather than trying to hide the emotional truth beneath a veneer of managerial bluster. This openness, however, has limits. If you're angry, you

must manage your anger so that you do not cause unintended and irreversible damage to the relationship and, possibly, your position in the organization.

3. *The "identity" conversation.* One of the reasons people feel threatened during a difficult conversation, with the associated emotions soon to follow, is that their identity, or at least their perception of how they are viewed by others, is being challenged. Most people view themselves as competent, and so when negative feedback about performance arrives, it usually collides with that self-image. Most people consider themselves honest, fair, and likable, and when that self-image is challenged, it cuts to the core of who they are or would like to be.

An awareness of all three levels as a conversation unfolds empowers you to understand the associated emotions on a deeper level. This enables you to address people in ways that prevent the raw emotion of the moment from clouding the issue at hand, at the same time earning you the respect that is given to executives who maintain a cool detachment in heated situations.

Preparing for a Difficult Conversation

Preparing to launch a difficult conversation involves more than simply having an idea about what you want to say. If your emotions are driving your urgency to face an issue with another person—in other words, if you are downright angry—perhaps you aren't as prepared as you should be. The strategy of conducting an effective conversation resides at its very core in managing the emotional component, including your own, so that you don't run the risk of taking a hit to your executive reputation.

A common mistake is to let issues and problems fester before they are faced. Although this may give you time to cool off and get your emotions in check, it is also a way of avoiding the issue. Avoidance means that the behavior or conditions that constitute the agenda of the conversation will go forward unaltered and unchecked, since the recipient has not heard your views. The consequences of that unwanted behavior—poor performance, a disruptive environment, safety compromises, and so on—will continue unabated until the issue is dealt with. Most of the time procrastination is a product of one's own anxiety and fear, and it is a trait that experienced and enlightened communicators—particularly those building a professional image—know they must overcome to optimize the impending discussion and its effect on the organization.

With this guideline as the context, here are the three stages of a process that can result in optimized conversations, no matter how difficult:

1. *Make sure you are clear about the issue.* You have all the facts, all the evidence, and all the implications well in hand. Make sure you have crafted the message you want to convey in the context of those facts.
2. *Don't hesitate.* Allow courage to override anxiety and the urge to put it off until another time.
3. *Execute the message.* Keep in mind that there are three levels of conversation unfolding simultaneously: what happened or needs to happen, the associated feelings, and the way the conversation challenges the other person's identity.

Clarity is critical to having a successful conversation. Simply telling someone that his work or attitude needs to improve is vague, and the emotions of the receiving party will cause him to build a wall of defensiveness immediately. Without clarity, he will try to make *you* appear wrong. Be specific about the exact behaviors and results you've seen that are less than acceptable and be clear about what you'd like to see instead. The more succinct a new goal that arises from the conversation is, the more likely it is that you'll see it come to pass.

The tendency to procrastinate isn't always about your fear of facing the issue. You may care about the other person's feelings, dreading telling her anything that may cause her to dislike you or challenge her self-image. However, just as a parent who withholds teaching from his child for fear that the child will throw a tantrum is not serving the child, managers must understand that feedback and mentoring are the best way to move employees toward the behaviors and attitudes they seek. Avoidance may not amount to cowardice, but it constitutes less than optimal performance on your part as a manager and won't help your quest to gain respect and assert your executive poise on the way to the corner office.

The execution of the conversation is the meat and potatoes of the challenge of having difficult encounters. It consists of two parts: *directness* and *sensitivity*. Too often a manager musters the courage to conquer her procrastination and then, powered by that self-induced head of steam, charges in with a directness that is delivered without sensitivity. Just as often, managers soft-pedal the issues to protect the employee's feelings, and the resultant message is less than direct. A middle ground is required, one that covers the three simultaneous conversations (what happened, feelings, and identity). Directness without sensitivity results in a message that may not be heard, since the recipient is protecting himself with defensiveness and resentment. However, if the message is delivered in a highly sensitive manner but with less than clear directness, the message probably will be heard but not understood completely. The middle ground—sometimes referred to as tough love—can be an optimal approach. Deliver a clear and direct message but never with brutal honesty, only crystal-clear honesty. If you do this with an awareness—and, most important, with *empathy*—of how the message feels and how it affects the person's self-image, you can adjust your approach to get the best of both objectives, not to mention adding some mixed metapoints to your scorecard in the marathon of executive excellence and leadership presence.

Finally, you must establish both directness and sensitivity as soon as possible in the discussion. Research shows that when this is accomplished in the first 30 seconds, the recipient remains open and the message gets through efficiently. If you start out by being too direct, the employee will shut you out reflexively, and if you start out by being too soft, he or she will not hear you in the way you intend.

Craft a Clear Objective to Make Your Conversations Stronger and Obtain Results

Once you're sure your emotions are in check, it can be helpful to prepare by creating an agenda for the impending conversation. Plot your opening, keeping the first 30 seconds in mind. Create context for the meat of the discussion by clarifying policies and cultural expectations that are already in place and can be juxtaposed against the issues you are about to address. Go through the issues in order of priority, from highest to lowest, so that each issue creates the context for the next. For example, if the issue is a salesperson who is habitually late for customer calls, begin there and show her how this creates a poor first impression and a negative context for the entire sales call. This puts other issues about the person's behaviors during those calls into a perspective that makes clearer sense and supports mutually held goals. Notice how this feels more like coaching than chastisement even though both may be your intention.

It can be effective to recognize the other person's point of view quickly. If in the above example you say that you realize the employee lives farther away than most of the other salespeople, you'll at least create a common understanding and eliminate that issue as a point of defense. If the person is being given feedback, say, on being a poor team player, recognize that the team is full of strong personalities and that others will be receiving feedback on their roles on the team as well. The effect is to create the context of you as an ally and mentor rather than an outsider and a disciplinarian. If we know anything about human nature, it's that people are more open to the wisdom of allies and mentors than to that of critics.

How to Deal with Emotional Outbursts and Negativity in Conversations

Of course, none of this may work as planned. Sometimes you can engineer all the negative feedback and outright criticism out of the conversation, but the feelings level within the discussion is always there, ready to respond when a raw nerve is touched. At that point you have very little control over the other party's response. However, you do have total control over your reaction to his or her response, and if you manage it effectively with an understanding of the executive presence you exude, you can minimize damage to the relationship and return the conversation to a productive realm.

There are two mistakes that are easy to make when someone across the table from you lashes out or allows his emotions to take control of him. One is to tell that person to calm down, to relax. In doing this you are in effect saying that his response is unwarranted, which is another way of saying that he is wrong. The other mistake is to match the person's emotions with you own, which is the quickest way to ignite a shouting match or, at a minimum, render the rest of the discussion dysfunctional.

Instead, stay calm. Hear her out. Recognize her emotions—"I know you're upset; I would be too if my boss just said that to me"—and demonstrate the empathy required to convey what you really want to say: "Calm down." An emotional outburst is a cry for attention, a signal of disconnection. She wants you to see how you've made her feel, so do just that, but with empathy—recognize the emotion as it happens.

When an emotional outburst occurs, the best response is to allow it to run its course. This may require a thick skin, and there may be a limit to the nature of the outburst, up to and including the matter of your safety and its appropriateness within your culture. Most of the time, though, if you let people have their say, you'll see their energy dissipate before your eyes, and the less defensive you are, the faster that will happen. Then, after an empathetic acknowledgment of what just happened, you can return to the discussion. If you can't get the moment under control, avoid the temptation to plow through; instead, abandon the discussion for the time being. When patience doesn't work, tell the other person that you'll continue when you can do so without the distraction of an outburst. Chances are that he or she will come to you first—and soon—if not with an apology, at least with an assurance that the outburst won't happen again.

How to Ask Questions That Build Receptivity and Trust

There is a big difference between a conversation and a lecture. The former is a matter of give and take, and when the conversation is difficult, it can be hard to get the other person to do either one. The key to making sure the conversation doesn't degenerate into a lecture—which will add little to your executive presence—is learning how to ask the right questions in the right way with a view to building trust and creating a positive, forward-looking context for the unfolding conversation. Questions are a way to allow the other person to tell his side of things, and if they are posed strategically, they can get the other person to explore your side of things. "Why do you think we ask people to observe those safety rules?" is better than asking, "Don't you understand those safety rules?" It's a subtle shift— "What do you want here" versus "How can I help you with this?"—that springs from a perspective of providing mentorship rather than criticism, even if the latter is part of the agenda. An enlightened communicator knows how to impart criticism in a way that feels like supportive mentoring rather than punishment. If you are at all emotional about the issue, it almost always will feel like punishment.

Whenever possible, your questions should be open-ended. Any question that requires a yes or no answer is closed-ended and does little to impart learning. The more you can get the employee's mind to process and explore what happened versus what should have happened and all the alternatives in between, the more cognitive and permanent the learning will be. Yes or no questions come from a lecturing and punishment approach, whereas a context of participation and teamwork arises from open-ended questions that by definition involve the employee in the creation of a solution. The former makes you a bully who's in charge; the latter, a leader whose executive presence is acknowledged, appreciated, and respected by employees and bosses alike.

Be careful, though, as you can go too far with questioning if the questions appear to be part of an interrogation rather than giving the clear impression of a give-and-take conversation. If the intention of your questions is to get the other person to admit his culpability or lack of knowledge, to him this can feel like getting grilled rather than being coached or mentored. Don't try to trick the person into admitting anything; if you believe there was an infraction, just say it. Then use conversation spiced with open-ended questions to explore the reasons behind the actions and the alternatives going forward.

Let's be clear: The intention here is not to manipulate the employee in any way. In fact, if your objectives and your style of delivery are not aligned, the other person will sense a disconnection and shut down, rendering the conversation ineffective and harming the executive image you're working to create. For example, if your intention is to reprimand someone—in effect, to punish her—with no agenda for understanding or moving forward with alternatives (this can happen, but rarely is punishment an effective incentive for change), your open-ended questions will come off as a means of humiliation. Then again, if your objective is truly to change behavior or impart learning, coming on too strong with negative feedback that hurts feelings and challenges identity will shut down the recipient's openness to the coaching and foster withdrawal and resentment. Your intentions need to be as clear as the facts you bring to the conversation, and you should do this not only with complete control of your emotions but with an understanding of how nonverbal cues—tone and volume of your voice, body language, use of pauses, and the like—contribute toward this clarity.

How to Use Body Language to Send a Message of Compassion, Empathy, and Respect

Effective Communication 101 teaches that when we convey an attitude, only a small fraction of what we perceive in conversation comes to us through the actual words used. That leaves the vast majority of meaning in the hands of other things, including tone of voice, volume, and body language: the way you stand or sit, cross your legs (or not), shift position, nod your head, move your eyes, and use your hands to emphasize your words. Most people do these things naturally, without conscious thought. When our emotions are involved, our adjustments are completely reflexive. However, if we want to optimize difficult conversations, especially ones that are emotionally tinged, we will be more effective when we *strategically* employ nonverbal cues, especially body language, as a tool rather than an involuntary reflex.

Nonverbal communication, especially body language, trumps words—when one conveys an attitude—when the two are in conflict as far as receiver perception is concerned. For example, you may state that you are not upset, but if your posture, the tightness in your face, and your clenched fists, combined with a tone and volume easily interpreted as barely restrained rage, are in conflict with what you've said, your words will be rendered meaningless. Conversely, when body language is in synch with your words, the total exceeds the sum of those parts.

Body language is more easily interpreted when you know the other person well. Assigning meaning to subtle body language in those we do not know well can be risky, since two people who are demonstrating the exact same tendency or reaction may have diametrically opposed meanings. If you know the person, body language can be gauged from a baseline of behavior and attitudes you are already familiar with, making your perception of meaning much closer to the mark. This is something to keep in mind as the provider of feedback in difficult conversations: Make sure that what you intend to say is reinforced by the way you carry yourself in the moment. In addition to being more effective in getting your message across clearly, you will exude a confidence that is vital to the overall executive presence you are establishing.

The most telling and meaningful form of nonverbal communications is eye contact. Not only is it intuitively obvious, research has shown that people trust and believe information delivered with sincere and unflinching eye contact more readily and deeply. Eye contact says not only that what you are saying is sincere but also that you're willing to listen in return, that you are present and engaged, even that you care. The eyes convey meaning—if you've ever had a significant other give you *the look*, you know this is true—and you can say volumes simply by the way you look at someone. Adjust your expression accordingly, since difficult conversations usually involve a roster of challenging moments that call for different levels of energy.

Another way to use body language to show sincerity is to nod occasionally as you listen. This shows that you are hearing and implies that you understand, perhaps approve. Take care, though, that you don't convey approval at the expense of honesty and intention. Use words to clarify the difference—a nod can say "I hear you" and "I understand you," whereas words can explain a different point of view on what you've just heard. Authenticity is the key here as even the slightest perception that you are only acting interested will lose you important points of respect from your counterparts, a loss that can lead to a less powerful executive presence in your run for business leadership.

Summarize Your Conversations for Maximum Impact and Positive Conclusions

People tend to hear what they want to hear. Sometimes what they hear isn't precisely what you intend to communicate. This is why all these techniques can improve effectiveness, since difficult conversations increase the likelihood of the other person hearing only what he wants to hear. One way to bridge this gap between intention and comprehension is to repeat back what you've just heard, paraphrasing and assigning meaning as you go. You can even ask the other person to do the same thing for what she's just heard from you. This is an excellent way to engage people in dialogue about the issue; there is no place to hide in response to such a request.

By definition, paraphrasing includes important details. In this case, repeat what you've heard in your own words without the details, sticking to a summarization of what you perceive to be the intended meaning. For example, someone may explain in sequence what actions she took during an accident on the factory floor. You then can play it back by saying something like "So what I heard you say is there was too much noise in the plant to hear other vehicles, and because you were in a hurry, you didn't see the cross traffic in that aisle." The other person can correct your summary according to her intended meaning, and you can meld that correction into your evolving perception of the issue.

Inviting feedback on what you've just summarized is an important part of the exchange, as it shows your evolving executive presence. This draws the other person into the dialogue, which is a dynamic of coaching that doesn't exist in lecturing and punishment. When the two of you agree on specific points, you have a basis on which to explore alternatives, establishing common ground on which to build for the future.

In Chapter 9 we'll discuss the importance of seeing yourself as a brand as you establish your executive presence and what you can do to make sure your brand is the one people choose.

PART III

A Brand Is a Promise: What Does Your Personal Brand Say?

9

Why Self-Branding Is No Longer a Choice and What Your Personal Brand Says about You

W E LIVE IN a society that defines itself through the phenomenon of branding. We rarely describe our favorite jeans by their color or style; we identify them — and their place in the social pecking order — by their brand. We do the same thing with our preferred coffee shops, cars, bars, computers, ketchup, peanut butter, phones, golf balls, restaurants, and even hospitals. Our grandfathers divided themselves into "Ford men" and "Chevy men," which is nothing more than the notion of branding manifesting as a middle-class colloquialism. Such groups still exist: You're into PCs or you're into Macs, and rarely do the twain meet, choose the same wardrobe, or even talk to each other.

This reliance on branding to fuel our self-image — and thus our buying decisions — is so pervasive that we cease to think of it as such. We don't use tissues; we wipe our noses with Kleenex. We move the earth with Caterpillars and Google new acquaintances on the Internet. Despite the protestations of the marketing pros at the companies whose names have been immortalized in this manner as generic, that nomenclature signals a status to which virtually all companies aspire. The name is synonymous with the product category, and thus, rightly or wrongly, those products define the standard. Any other product in that niche, no matter how well reviewed or how large its share of the market, is an also-ran.

Certain brands may not be quite at that level but nonetheless have an anointed status that may or may not relate to the quality of their products. Harvard, Stanford, and MIT are branded as institutions of unreproachable standards of quality; they are regarded as more prestigious than other learning institutions that deliver the same level of education. Virtually every product niche has a branded front-runner in terms of prestige and reputation, and the primary explanation, over and above quality and value, is the brand that has been developed. However, branding is not confined to corporate names and product positioning. The phenomenon has become personal, and therein, because of the technologies at our disposal, resides an opportunity that perhaps was unavailable to our Ford- or Chevy-loyal forebears but is within reach for business professionals who are looking to create their own unique brand of executive presence.

The Difference between Random Branding and Controlled Branding

What exactly is a brand? People think of a brand as something that has a locked file cabinet full of design trademarks and copyrights and a suite of lawyers on call to protect and defend them. Brands appear to be something that required hordes of specialists years to develop at a cost often measured in the hundreds of millions of dollars. That perception is not completely wrong: Brands don't just happen; they are the sum of everything that goes into the delivery of quality, the positioning and marketing of products and services, and over time the achieving of a tipping point in terms of word-of-mouth, on-the-street reputation. The goal of achieving the status of cool or elite or safe is more art than science yet is supported by carefully devised strategy and immense investment.

The lion's share of the investment in branding is in the form of advertising. If you watch the Super Bowl, you will see the most expensive advertisements imaginable in terms of media buys (not necessarily in terms of production budget) that strive not so much to pitch us product features and benefits as to increase our awareness of a brand. Hip-talking toddlers, junior execs flying out of windows, and dancing lizards say little about how a product stacks up yet speak volumes about the essence of the brand. A few decades ago there was only one car rental brand on the planet (Hertz), but when Avis came up with its "we're number two, we try harder" campaign, suddenly there was a new brand on the block: same type of company, same service, but a new perception.

These are all *controlled branding* strategies. You've never seen a Nike commercial that wasn't exceedingly hip and cool or a political ad that wasn't overtly spun. This is a case of brand trumping product, because savvy marketers know that perception is everything. Beyond advertising and public relations, though, all that's left is the largely uncontrollable element of public preference and taste, and because that is a sum of variables that are largely out of our control, the best a company or individual can do is to seize momentum and create opportunities to put the brand out there keeping a steady focus on quality, reputation, competition, and perception. Without a brand, a product must fend for itself, and research shows that that is usually not enough. Without a brand, good products, great ideas, and talented people sink beneath a crowded sea of mediocrity as a matter of course.

Although we don't tend to think of it this way, the phenomenon of branding is just as pervasive and influential for individuals. This applies not just to celebrities and politicians—who, like products, employ professionals to mold, spin, and propel their brand into the marketplace—but to anyone who is seeking to build a career, a reputation, a social network, or a perception on the part of the public of executive presence. No matter how narrow a segment they are targeting, they want to show that they are worthy, talented, or downright cool.

Famed business tycoons such as Donald Trump, Martha Stewart, Oprah Winfrey, Steve Jobs, and Richard Branson owe their ascent to executive presence and instant recognition as much to successful branding as to the viability of their products and the weight of their experience. These superstars of business and the media managed to attach their names and likenesses to a variety of services and products that are virtually inseparable in the public's collective mind from the founders of the business. Each one is unique in the brand he or she has created, and in all cases their executive presence is palpable. They command respect from a global audience not only because of their superior products but because they understand the power of creating a strong presence that connects emotionally and intellectually with their constituents. When you hear their names and see their faces, you instantly know what they stand for. This instant recognition of one's strengths and character should be your goal as you strive to create your own executive presence.

The notion that everyone already has created a personal brand may be surprising. Some people have a brand that is compelling and positively differentiating, whereas others lack distinction, which in and of itself is a type of branding (think Morton's versus Applebee's). People manifest and shape their personal brands each and every day they show up for work, including the kind of car they leave in the lot, the way they dress, the way they carry themselves and greet others, and the way they do their work. Many people *randomly* create a personal brand without a plan and without the slightest awareness of the power of branding to penetrate the sensiblities of those around them, for better or for worse. If you consistently show up late for meetings and your presentations lack substance, if you're generally serious or unpleasant, by default you're creating a personal brand. If you feed others at work by always bringing baked goods for everyone to share, if you know the names of your coworkers' children and ask about their lives, you're also creating a personal brand that stays with you when the social niceties give way to doing business.

This goes beyond personality and energy: If it's you everybody turns to when the computer goes down, you've created a personal brand that says you are the one to turn to when the screen goes blank. Whether your brand *serves* you, however, is another issue altogether. It's easy to create a random brand: You don't give the way you're perceived any thought and just take your chances. However, to ensure the respect of your peers, employees, and bosses and eventually the general public by using the power of branding to further your career and personal goals, you want to use a *controlled* approach to the art and craft of branding that is every bit as effective and rewarding as the strategies employed on Madison Avenue.

Start Thinking in Terms of My Executive Presence, Inc.

One way to approach the process of branding yourself—and this includes evolving or completely overhauling the random brand you've already created—is to think of yourself as a corporation in which you are the CEO. This entails being keenly aware of everything you put out there, from your appearance to your social energy to the way you conduct yourself on the job. When that awareness is matched with an understanding of how you are perceived by others and what that perception means in terms of how you are valued and the degree to which you exert legitimate influence (versus fear), you are equipped to take your brand to new heights.

In business and in life, we like to think that we create our own breaks, go after what we want, and earn our respective fates. However, the truth is—and this is something every great achiever will endorse—you have to put yourself in the way of approaching opportunity. You need to create a pathway on which luck will walk into your life. Your personal brand—your executive presence—is the primary element of the process of attracting good fortune or what others perceive to be pure blind luck.

A popular New Age take on this was promulgated in the movie and book called *The Secret,* in which we are advised to think exclusively positive thoughts and manifest nothing but positive energy. This involves a vivid visualization of what we desire, including our wildest dreams, so that the positive vibrations we broadcast to the universe will attract the equally positive energy that is—according to the theory—floating around in the ether in search of a landing pad. This is nothing more than opening the door to opportunity and attracting those opportunities through an effective personal brand, because people do business with people they like and admire. They also promote those people, give them raises, invite them to cool functions, and think of them first when something important and exciting is put on the table. Personal branding is the process of becoming that kind of person, and you get there by managing each and every moment of your day toward that end. If you want to call it a secret, be my guest; I prefer to think of it as effective personal branding.

Consider respected athletes who happen to play for less than stellar teams. Although attendance dwindles as their teams sink to the bottom of the standings, their personal brands are insulated by their performance. Here we're talking about not only on-the-field results but also their presence, character, integrity, and energy in general. Just ask Michael Vick and Michael Phelps what happens to a personal brand when a person's energy is not congruent with his or her athletic ability. The same is true for all of us: Job performance is only one element in the branding process. Your brand is not just what you can do; it is a sum that includes how you do it and who you are in the process. It is the power of that sum total, its ability to influence choices and consequences, that can make you stand out. As the CEO of My Executive Presence, Inc., you have the power to hire, fire, promote, and support each facet of your being. If you do it right, people will notice. You'll have developed a brand and a charismatic executive presence that will serve you going forward.

How to Develop Yourself into a Compelling Brand

The first rule of branding is to be proactive in controlling everything about the way you are perceived so that you do not allow random branding—decisions, actions, and attitudes that are allowed to remain unmanaged and unaccountable—to define you. Successfully branded companies do it—they have entire departments full of highly paid branding specialists—because they understand not only that the competition is doing the same thing but that taking your brand for granted leaves the job to the fickle perceptions of the market, where your product alone may not be enough to occupy valuable mind space in your constituents, tilting decision making in your favor.

One of the places where branding—both for companies and for individuals—is critical and in full bloom is on the Internet. More and more people are consulting the Internet before making a final decision, and that means your site—again, as a company or an individual—is the first and often the primary billboard for your brand. In Chapter 10 we'll look specifically at branding on the Internet and explain how you can take advantage of the latest technology to make yourself stand out and assert a compelling executive poise.

Despite the new context of technology, we tend to think of branding as product- or company-specific even in the face of the need to brand ourselves personally. The closest the corporate world comes to being a model for personal branding is seen in the services industry, in which consultants and tax firms compete for mind share by using their reputations—their brands. Price is rarely the issue, nor is a referral or an advertisement. With these constraints, all we have to work with is our character and our performance as viewed through the lens of perception of others. Firms that violate the limits of tolerance take a hit to their brands—think Arthur Andersen and, more recently, a horde of fun-loving politicians whose names appeared in the wrong black book—and it's not long before the consequences manifest themselves. The same thing is true for us as individuals: We are how we are perceived.

The secret to branding yourself either as a service company or as an individual working in a culture full of other well-dressed, really smart people with BlackBerry thumbs is to *distinguish* yourself, to separate yourself from the crowd in a way that serves you. The first questions to ask in that area are these: What makes you unique? How are you special? In what ways are you different from your peers? What do you have to offer that they don't? This should always be a positive analysis—judging others as less capable isn't the way to create an effective brand—that delivers promise and value, but never at anyone else's expense.

Are you the person who always gets things done first? The one who has the most off-the-wall ideas that turn out to be effective? The one who spends the least to achieve the most? The one others turn to for advice and support? The first one in and the last one to leave? Are you a sure thing in a field in which nothing is sure? Are you unfailingly reliable, enthusiastic, flexible, coachable, helpful, and careful? Do you finish strong? The answers to these questions are the stuff of your personal brand, and the way you put them out there is to *live* them, to *be* them, as opposed to announcing them. When you live the essence of your brand and do it without stepping on toes or offending the sensibilities of others, a positive perception soon will follow even if the old you branded yourself as something else entirely.

The Steps to Personal Branding

It's easy to perceive the process of personal branding as a theory, a set of social and psychological principles that quickly blur around the edges. It's sort of like dieting and fitness, and we all know how well they work over the long term. However, when you reduce the process of personal branding and executive presence building to a sequence of steps and checklists, a road map emerges that will lead you to higher places in your career and your personal life:

- Recognize that you could be doing better in your career, in your personal life, and in general, that you want something more. Commit to improving things by creating a personal brand that better serves you.
- Announce to yourself the launch of My Executive Presence, Inc., an enterprise devoted to excellence and advancement through competence, service, and the manifesting of positive energies and behaviors. Name yourself the CEO and write a job description to which you will be held accountable. (If feasible, find yourself a qualified executive coach to whom you can be accountable.)
- Decide to move from random branding to controlled branding in your life. Declare that My Executive Presence, Inc., is open for business (as opposed to the launch phase, which is focused on planning and strategy) and that as a sophisticated CEO and marketer of your product (yourself), you understand the importance of branding to the success of the enterprise.
- Assess the nature and status of your existing personal brand, however randomly you may have created it. How are you perceived, and what actions, deeds, or energies have you manifested that have resulted in this perception of you? Ask for feedback from trusted sources and be open to hearing things you may not expect or like.
- Identify specific changes in attitude, behavior, techniques, character, and general energy that will strengthen your brand and reinforce your executive presence. Then commit to them.

Forgive yourself for imperfection as you move forward one day at a time, always doing the best you can to live your new brand.

- What makes you unique? What do you have to offer that sets you apart in your personal marketplace (in essence, your company or social group)? Develop a strategy that plays to your strengths and applies them to creating and implementing solutions, to being of value, to helping others and generally bringing your unique selling proposition (in this case your new brand) to your personal marketplace.

- Market yourself. That's right, put yourself out there and make sure people understand the new you—your new brand. Don't brag, don't announce, but be strategic about seizing new opportunities, modalities, and patterns that will manifest your new brand. When you hit enough home runs, the other players will notice.

- Understand that everything matters. Just as with a company and its brand, every stock-keeping unit, every service, every ad, every sale, every display, every press release, and the appearance of every employee and building play a part in establishing the brand. The same thing goes for you and the perception of your executive image.

- Continue the feedback-gathering and self-assessment process as you make adjustments along the way. Give yourself regular performance reviews, with identified adjustments as required.

- Discover your personal power. This has nothing to do with title and position; it has everything to do with credibility and influence. A strong brand exerts influence; a weak one doesn't. The kind of power that demonstrates that you can influence people is the point of it all. Once you have it, you need to use it to build your brand. How? By taking the lead, walking the walk, stepping up, volunteering, breaking down old barriers, and expanding your role. Use your power to make others successful, if not through overt support, then by example. Do the hard work, the stuff from which others hide.

- It's not your father's world anymore. What used to be a corporate ladder is now a checkerboard that borders on being a maze. This world is defined by projects in a way that is anything but linear. The best you can do, the most you can expect, is to create wins one project at a time. Hit it out of the park and then move on to the next project with the same expectation and personal brand, because that's how you roll.

- Stay the course. You may become the living embodiment of your new brand quickly (or not), but rest assured, it will take time for others to notice, especially if a shift in perception is required. The old saying "You never get a second chance to make a first impression" applies here, and so your goal should be to shift perception toward your newly branded self rather than to ghosts of the past. It's all about word of mouth, and that process takes time.

- Grow as you go. Things change; no two projects are alike these days. Don't hesitate to adjust your personal branding strategy accordingly, keeping what works and revising what doesn't.

- Enjoy the ride. Good things will happen to you when you stick to your commitment to yourself regardless of the time it takes. You'll find you have a new awareness of everything, especially the consequences of your actions, behaviors, and decisions, that will empower you to reach your goals as never before. If you're not having fun, people will notice that too, and your newly branded executive presence will suffer for it.

What to Do When Your Personal Brand Takes a Hit

There is a big difference between rebuilding or reinventing a personal brand and starting from scratch. Unless you just stepped off the moving van in a new city or have been transferred to a completely different cubicle farm somewhere in the corporate wasteland, your randomly forged personal brand precedes and defines you, adding context to everything you do. It is rare to build a brand from a zero base (again, unless you are arriving in a new environment, working with people who don't know you); there are almost always preconceptions—if not baggage—to work around.

The headlines are full of people with familiar names who are taking hits to their personal brands faster than a blind guy in a cage fight. An example would be the rocket scientists running the auto giants who traveled to Washington in separate private jets—at about a hundred times the cost of a commercial ticket—to beg Congress for bailout money. Incidentally, the bad press they received for that Marie Antoinette–style faux pas apparently wasn't educational enough, as we saw when Ken Lewis, Bank of America's CEO, responded to a subpoena by New York State Attorney General Cuomo by flying in the BoA corporate jet to the interview to the tune of $5,000 an hour. Then there are the PR dropouts from AIG who after cashing their bailout check took the management gang to a resort for golf and cocktails on the taxpayers' dollar. After taking relentless blows to his executive presence, John Thain—the CEO of a badly limping Merrill Lynch who spent $1.2 million redecorating his office—isn't likely to emerge soon on the good side of public perception. When Michael Phelps got his picture snapped with a bong clamped over his face, he was only one of many examples of personal brand busting from the world of athletics.

All these people had a personal brand that they thought was working just fine, and because of the public's perception of their respective falls from grace—or, perhaps better put, their stepping into a steaming pile of their own cluenessness—those brands are forever—or at least for a good while—tarnished. With that went their crediblity, the loyalty of those who were followers and admirers, and, in Phelps's case, millions of dollars in endorsement money.

However, Phelps has become the poster boy for how to weather a PR debacle. Without the slightest trace of confusion or indignation, he copped to the reality and fessed up, and he did so with genuine humility that bordered on grace. With a $100 million windfall of personal income over the next 10 years hanging in the balance, he took responsibility for what he'd done, apologized from the heart, and pledged to work harder not only to succeed in his sport but to remain worthy of the trust and support of those he had disappointed. He took the medicine of his three-month suspension without comment (other than saying he thought it was fair), and most of his sponsors have decided to give him a second shot. Instead of directing their scorn and resentment at him, most people are rooting for him to succeed.

If your brand takes a hit because of an isolated mistake on your part or the perception of one, your only chance of recovery lies in owning up to your part in it. True leaders assume accountability for their teams, and because you are the leader of My Executive Presence, Inc., this is expected of you when you fall. If your brand is tarnished because of poorly executed random behavior—you are perceived as an arrogant jerk who grabs all the credit—the strategy is twofold: (1) walk the walk and (2) talk the talk. You need to be different going forward, and you need to sound different. If you were arrogant and insensitive, you need to be humble and fully aware of the way others perceive you. A new branding strategy is nothing short of a reinvention of yourself (not to be confused with a reinvention of how others perceive you; the latter is effect, and the former is cause), and when you start down that road, even in the shadow of some transgression, you can never look back, at least if you hope to see your new personal brand emerge.

In Chapter 10 we'll continue to look at branding and go more deeply into the issue of how to build your brand on the Internet as you craft a powerful executive presence that tells others instantly who you are and what you stand for.

10

Branding 2.0: How to Use the Internet to Build and Expand Your Personal and Professional Brand

Dane Cook: A Case Study on How Real-World Superstars Are Created Online

How many friends do you have? I mean friends who laugh at all your jokes and show up whenever you throw a party, excited to see you and never coming empty-handed.

Dane Cook has over 2 million, give or take, and they've made him very wealthy. Cook, one of the most successful comedians today, is one of a number of real-world superstars who reached critical mass online—with a little help from his friends.

Let's start with some quick history on this unlikely Internet legend. Having done stand-up for a number of years, touring various clubs and the college circuit around the country, Cook decided to create an online presence. He put up a cheap Web site in 1999 that basically served as an advertisement for his comedy gigs. Traffic was slow and visitors to the site were few, yet although his online marketing barely had a pulse, onstage Cook was getting regular gigs and becoming a staple on cable's Comedy

Central. So far, nothing unusual. Lots of comics have gone the same route: smoky clubs, rowdy college bars, and, if they were lucky and very talented, a few appearances on Letterman or Leno.

After his onstage success, the hits and visitors to Cook's fledgling Web site started to increase. Gradually, the Dane Cook brand began to show promise of expanding its influence via the cyber world. Sensing the potential for more immediate benefits by establishing a direct relationship with his fans, Cook reportedly emptied his bank account and put it all into the design and building of an e-commerce site with his name, danecook.com, where people could buy merchandise, watch his videos, and get performance dates and all kinds of personal information about him. For Cook it was only the beginning of the legendary Internet-rags-to-riches story that surrounds him. Since that time he has starred in major motion pictures, sold out Madison Square Garden—only the second comic to do so—and won numerous awards for his edgy brand of comedy.

Phase 2 of Cook's Internet success began when the skyrocketing social online network MySpace was launched in 2003. Cook again showed his vision by creating a personal page on the site weeks before the social networking giant went live, linking it to his amped-up e-commerce site danecook.com. The rest is history, as Cook used his MySpace account to recruit 2.5 million friends, creating legions of followers and fans that grew by leaps and bounds as they anticipated his new jokes and then forwarded them along with videos of his stand-up routines to others, organically recruiting more and more fans as time went on.

Former HBO boss Chris Albrecht said this about Cook in an interview in *Forbes* magazine in 2006: "Dane has used the Internet to create and maintain a unique relationship with his audience." He went on to say: "It's a way for people to spread the word about Dane among themselves, as opposed to someone trying to advertise their way into a fan base."

Cook's shows sell out quickly these days mainly because of his very personal dialogue with his fans online. They feel that he's one of them, online on a social networking site the way they are, keeping it real. To say that his online friends are a captive audience would be a massive understatement. They're more like his disciples, spreading his gospel far and wide among everyone they know and chat with on the Web. For his part, Cook keeps the conversation alive, leaving messages on his site, telling jokes, and promoting his gigs on MySpace to millions of his closest friends, comfortable in the knowledge that the adoring masses will show up wherever and whenever he plays.

So what did this thirtysomething comedian do right when so many others—really smart others who study branding and do it for a living— have struggled to build a compelling brand, take it online, and grow it into a phenomenon the way Cook did? You'll learn all about it next.

How to Take Advantage of Social Networking Sites Such as MySpace and Facebook to Promote Your Brand

Type "social media" into Google and you'll get 30 million search results.

If you're not familiar with how social media work and how they have revolutionized and democratized communication on the Web, I encourage you to put the book down now. Then call everyone you know under age 50 and ask them to show you their Facebook or MySpace sites—they will have them—over a cup of coffee. Have them take you through their sites and show you all the cool features and gadgets and ways to link and connect with old friends and new friends.

But before you dive headfirst into creating your own page, finish reading this book. You'll have a much better understanding of how these social networking sites can enhance or destroy someone's reputation and help build a powerful personal brand or derail one's best efforts from the start.

Smart marketers such as Dane Cook understand and embrace the idea that the methods of traditional brand management as the primary way to connect with consumers are passé. To establish a powerful presence in the hearts and minds of people and gain the respect of ever-growing groups of those with like minds, the practice of imposing your presence, ideas, products, services, and opinions on others who seem to fit a certain profile is played out.

Brand management worked, as we hinted in Chapter 9, before MySpace, Facebook, YouTube, and other social media began, by unleashing top marketing professionals onto a product (I include "branded" personalities in the product category here, for example, winners on *American Idol*, top athletes, authors, business tycoons such as Donald Trump) or service to give it a unique identity designed to increase its perceived value and appeal to the end user or follower. When the branding process was given emotional salience via packaging, advertising, commercials, jingles, slogans, and recognizable spokespersons—often celebrities—the end result process was a high-stakes (at a high cost) gamble that consumers would bond with the heavily branded product and choose it over competing products that didn't create the same strong impressions and were left on the proverbial shelf.

Once the marketers had gained the trust of consumers with implied promises of quality, consistency, and other emotional rewards that encouraged future purchases of a product, they had to maintain this mind and market share with hundreds of millions of dollars of messaging via advertising and publicity. The consumer, drawn emotionally into the stories told in commercials and packaging, believing the celebrity spokesperson, and experiencing the superior value of the brand, didn't mind spending a little more for the experience or giving his or her valuable time to the venue in which a brand presented itself.

The problem with this model is that it doesn't always work and that even when it does, it is a prohibitively expensive and time- and labor consuming proposition. It's a high-stakes gamble with untold numbers of losers littering the archives and storage areas of advertising and PR companies and clients who didn't go broke in the process and therefore still had a storage area.

Fortunately for those who aren't NBC, Coca-Cola, Microsoft, or Procter & Gamble, the rules of engagement have changed. A big part of the change is that the Internet and social media have made it easier than ever to connect with people who want to buy what you're selling.

Dane Cook serves as a powerful example of how social media, with their low barriers to entry, can be used effectively to build a powerful personal brand that business professionals can leverage to create a power-boosting executive presence. While building and honing his real-world presence and connecting to his customers via promoters, cable television, and traditional advertising, Cook figured that he could establish a more authentic and intimate connection by having a real dialogue with his fans and placing himself in their midst, and so he moved into a virtual dorm room in the same virtual building where they were: MySpace.com. He joined people in their chat rooms, communicating on their wavelength and discussing topics that interested and moved them. Their rooms were off limits to big corporate marketing tactics, but Dane just told them a few jokes. He also let them look at his videos if they wanted to. No pressure. They were there for the viewing whenever viewers felt like it: Have fun. Tell your friends.

People started wanting a lot more of Dane Cook—funny guy—and if they clicked over to his other site, the e-commerce site, they'd find T-shirts, CDs, DVDs, downloads, and video clips that they could buy. No one felt manipulated or pressured, because hey, Dane's a friend and you're just checking out his stuff. Because they liked what he had to offer and he established trust without selling them, they gave him the permission to tell them about concert dates and other stuff he had for sale. Plus, his jokes and videos gave people great reasons to connect with one another. Sharing the clips and audio of prank phone calls allowed people to laugh together and bond over Cook's wares.

What Dane did that is different from traditional brand management in building his brand is that he figured out who his most likely friends would be and who would love—not like but love—his sense of humor. He also figured out where they were in droves. He then tapped into a like-minded—they're all on MySpace, after all—group of people who all had very similar characteristics and preferences, and instead of pushing something down their throats with traditional methods, he simply gave people a reason to share his sense of humor.

The term that best describes the new model of online brand management that Cook demonstrated is *tribe management*, a definition widely attributed to marketer, bestselling author, and blogger Seth Godin, who wrote a compelling book on the topic titled *Tribes*.

What enlightened brand builders such as Dane Cook have gathered is that to deliver your messages to people who expect them, are open to them, and are interested in what you have to say, you have to be allowed in first. Once they agree to let you into their lives, you can help them connect—which is what they really want—to like-minded others for which you and your brand become a powerful conduit, to everyone's benefit.

Think of Harley-Davidson and the tribes that have formed around that powerful brand. It may be fun to ride a "Fat Boy" Softail around town by oneself, but it doesn't compare with the thrill of connecting with other riders and touring several states together or congregating by the thousand in Sturgis, South Dakota, every year. The true definition of a tribe, Harley-Davidson fans express themselves and show their tribal affiliation with their black leather gear, Harley-Davidson's orange logo, and their bandanas, sunglasses, and other markings. They are bartenders, accountants, pet-shop owners, financial analysts, truck drivers, and lawyers with different backgrounds and socioeconomic levels, but all are part of a strong tribe created by the brand.

It follows that people love hearing from the company or the person—the brand—because they know they're part of a community or tribe. They know that the brand connects them and gives them a reason to talk to one another; to exchange stories, gossip, and ideas; and to build lasting relationships that give back more than they could receive without being part of the tribe. What's true for Harley-Davidson's tribes is just as true for many other brands' tribes, such as those of Harvard Business School, Steve Jobs—an extension of the Apple brand—the TED conference, Tony Robbins, NASCAR, the Boston Red Sox, Oprah, the Rolling Stones, Google, and, for now at least, Barack Obama.

Your challenge in creating a personal or professional brand through social media and by fashioning your executive presence is to reposition yourself, your products, and your services in the way people want them; then those people want to share the experience with others, for which the social networking culture is a superhighway. Find a way that people can have a visceral experience that is based on what they perceive from you and you'll have their attention.

Before you make boring videos that are scripted and produced by your marketing department by the dozens and post them on YouTube, reconsider. Who's going to watch a boring company advertisement—no matter how clever you think your little stories are—when there is a company showing videos of blenders that have taken blending to an extreme level? The brand is Blendtec, and its videos are famous on YouTube, having blended everything from German-to-English dictionaries, to personal navigation systems, to iPhones.

Their slogan is "Will it blend?" and in showing their blenders' superior quality, the makers of the Blendtec brand have figured out a way to connect people to one another and talk and enthuse about a most unlikely topic of conversation among friends: a kitchen appliance—a blender!

The traps in building brands are boredom, irrelevance, and lack of emotional experience among one's constituents. Overcome that and give people something that causes a strong emotional response that makes them want to share their experiences with others and you're on your way to creating your own tribe, in the process building and reinforcing the emotional bonds that make up your personal and professional brand.

The Future Is Archived: How to Build a Consistent Brand That Keeps Building on Itself

If we embrace the notion that a brand at its core is a promise to a constituency that cares, we have to get used to the fact that it is easier than ever to break that promise in an increasingly transparent world.

From business-related considerations such as profit and loss, to human nature, to economic interference, some of the brands we ambitiously work to create have the life expectancy of a fruit fly. From angry recorded rants, to compromised values, to unfavorable market conditions—all things that can cause a brand to disintegrate—everyone will know why, when, and how it all fell apart.

The brands we create for others to notice and respond to emotionally will be manifest on the Internet for all to see and evaluate, for better or worse.

How can we build a consistent personal brand online, where each message the brand sends serves as the foundation for the next message? Here are some ideas that can contribute to the strength of your executive presence:

Be Authentic

Don't pretend to be something you are not. You won't be able to keep up the act for very long. Once people see through insincerity, it's over. They will lose trust and become cynical. It's like getting stained by expensive packaging where the ink rubs off. We feel cheated. Just ask the former New York governor Elliot Spitzer. His double life unraveled when he betrayed the rock-solid principles everyone thought he stood for when he was caught hiring prostitutes, irreparably damaging his perceived incorruptible brand as the white knight of Wall Street. Think of the loss of trust the Catholic Church suffered after widespread allegations of the sexual abuse of children by priests. Being authentic means doing a thorough inventory of who you are and then deciding whether you can live that as part of your brand. If your values and those of your brand don't match, do something else. The Internet is unforgiving, and your transgressions will be posted and archived, perhaps crippling your brand permanently and preventing you from ever achieving your true potential via a solid executive presence.

Be Likable

If you're likable, you will find that nice things—not in all cases; everyone has a critic—will be written about you and the brand you have created. The more nice things are said about you online on blogs, chat rooms, and news articles and editorials, the more you'll have the benefit of the doubt when someone is less than cordial toward you. You'll have automatic defenders among your tribe—if you're likable.

Overdeliver

Always do more than what's expected. The effort alone will pay dividends. If you make it part of your modus operandi, everyone will take notice. It will leave tracks online in terms of customer comments, testimonials, and endorsements.

Stand for Something

Warren Buffett stands for something. So does FedEx. Ditto for Steve Jobs and Google. AT&T? It's getting a little fuzzy, and the same thing goes for AOL. When people get confused about what you stand for, it's time to regroup and think of a message that will create trust again. Vagueness doesn't work for a brand, and it doesn't help reinforce the executive presence you're trying to create in the minds of coworkers, employees, and bosses.

Be Timely

Has it been a while since people have heard from you personally? Maybe you're not around anymore. If you are, keep sending those messages. When there's a gap in communication, people tend to fill it in with bias, speculation, and rumor, particularly on blogs. Also, people like to be kept in the loop. They want to be part of a conversation. If you've branded yourself with a tribe and earned the respect executive presence gets you, keep the connection strong and the lines of communication open. See in the final section of this chapter how several visionary CEOs practice staying in touch with their constituents.

Be Unpredictable

Do this in a good way, of course. When Bill Gates opened a jar of mosquitoes at a recent TED conference, the reaction was first shock, then amusement. It was powerful and positive. He made a strong point about malaria, and the Internet was buzzing (no pun intended) about it. Gates reinforced the perception of his commitment to fighting the disease in third world countries.

Create a Culture

There is no point doing all you can to maintain the integrity of your brand when other stakeholders are pulling in a different direction. From the most remote frontline employee all the way to the CEO, the message that comes from your brand has to be consistent or you will lose the trust and weaken the presence you've worked so hard to build. The weakest link will make the biggest impression, and it will be that link that is most newsworthy. The news will be unusual and unexpected, but in a bad way.

Get Involved

Create a scholarship. Establish a charity. Champion a cause. The more you get involved in making this planet a better place, the more reciprocal response you will see online and offline. Find out what bothers people and what issues matter most to them. Step in to help and your brand will benefit from the warm glow of your good deeds. When people check your history online to see where you were when help was needed, you can point to the results with confidence.

Be Accessible

Sometimes people need to complain. Make that easy to do. It's become a bit of a cliché that a customer's complaint is your greatest gift because it allows you to wow that customer and make the connection stronger. You decide whether the cliché is true. Give people as many ways to get in touch with you as possible: message boards you monitor, blogs where they can leave a comment, 800 numbers, and plenty of customer service reps with on-hold times less than 2 minutes. Let them vent with you before they do it online. Fix their issues quickly, and their subsequent online response may turn into a boon for you.

Keep Your Promises

Break promises even once and you'll get caught. The Internet is unforgiving and remembers everything. Politicians in general have low trust and approval ratings because they tend to make vast promises to get elected that they're later forced to go back on. That is not a good way to build a brand. Remember, the future is archived.

How to Keep Your Brand Humming Online

Your brand lives by the attention it gets and the reputation it has online. It's noisier than ever on the Web—from advertisements for the latest get-rich-quick schemes to a myriad of product- and service pitches invading our screens via annoying pop-up ads to news and blogs from thousands of channels, sordid entertainment stories about who's hooked up with whom, and YouTube videos that show drunken Japanese finance ministers. Hundreds of e-mails accumulate over a busy day of meetings away from the computer. Who has time to pay attention to you and your brand?

You need to stand out from the noisy online crowd, and to do that you need principles. The ideas discussed next will help you start thinking strategically about how you can keep your brand from flatlining online and consistently carve out a little mind share in an attention-deficit-plagued society.

Innovation Matters

Steve Jobs gets it, and so should you. The Apple impresario keeps the buzz going about new developments in the iPhone, the iPod, and laptops thinner than a slice of cheese. He does this by consistently coming up with unexpected new product features and designs. The resulting chatter keeps Jobs and Apple in the conversation and in the black. To keep pace with society's fleeting attention spans and fickle tastes we have to do the same thing with our brands. Never rest; always think about ways to innovate and develop buzzworthy conversation starters. If your fans, customers, followers, clients, voters, and other constituents aren't excited about you anymore, they'll stop talking about you. Putting all your creative energy into improving what was hot about you yesterday—or five minutes ago on the Internet—will pay off when you're the topic of discussion again today.

Keep Talking

You want the world to talk about you, and so you have to do a lot of talking yourself. It's called a conversation, and who better to tell your raving fans you want to hear from them than you, the brand? The Internet's hierarchy is flat, and people don't want to talk to a marketing person or a customer service rep or some other hired gun who speaks for you. Get on the other site of the monitor, cut out the person in the middle, and start talking to your customers. It's time-consuming and fraught with risk—you don't want to spill the beans about a merger that was supposed to be hush-hush—but the fewer layers people have to wade through to hear it from the horse's mouth, the less BS and spin they feel they're getting. CEOs who have gained the respect of their tribes and strengthened their executive presence by being chief communicators for their brands include Zappo.com's Tony Hsieh, GoDaddy.com CEO and founder Bob Parsons, and Craigslist founder Craig Newmark. Even Donald Trump has a blog on his Trump University site where he dishes on everything from his frequent on-air interviews with Larry King to his ideas on how entrepreneurs can prosper in a volatile economy—always imbued with the Donald's unique executive presence. They tweet, they blog, they talk to their fans, and that's the way you keep the relationship fresh and your brand in the minds of your customers.

Present Well

Your Web site or portal or whatever it is that people get to first that is your home on the Web should be spectacular. I don't mean spectacular like your neighbor's annual Christmas display that could power the Chrysler Building. It should be spectacular as in simple, elegant, and ultra-user-friendly: easy to navigate, easy to figure out, and easy to find what one's looking for. Rather than pen a tutorial on what a persuasive Web site looks like, I'll have you skip over to Apple.com and have a look for yourself. It's just one example of many uncluttered and friendly sites that tell visitors who they're dealing with and what the experience might be like. Unfortunately, for every site that offers the online equivalent of a firm handshake and a smile, there are thousands that are the cyber equivalent of a burp in the face and a grunted "What's up?" In rare instances that is intentional, such as with a punk rock band, but your brand lives online 24/7, and each visitor who comes to your site will walk away—via the back button—with an impression of whether the relationship has potential.

In Chapter 11 we'll start looking at the perils and opportunities in the age of 24-hour media and how the media determine the meaning of many of the messages that come at us. You'll learn how spin works and how you can use it to your advantage in creating an executive presence.

PART IV

THE AGE OF 24-HOUR MEDIA: IF YOU'RE NOT ON, YOU'RE OUT

11

How the Media Create Meaning in the Minds of an Audience: Powerful Messages and the Art of Spin

---

MODERN BUSINESS EXECUTIVES have to be ready to speak for their company, their brand, and themselves when opportunity—or pressing need—comes knocking. In this chapter you'll learn techniques and secrets for defining your message successfully and communicating it powerfully so that it will connect with your public. We'll also spend time talking about the media and PR's dirty little secret—the art of spinning—and what it means for you. First, let's look at what my colleagues and I tell our clients who are about to go public.

Top Communications Professionals Share Their Strategies

What are reporters really after in an interview? How can you speak to the media in a way that will get your most important messages into the news? With input from some of the country's most sought after PR experts, experienced journalists, and other communications professionals, I've designed a deceptively simple three-part strategy. It can form the basis of a plan that can be used by all individuals looking to boost their visibility via executive presence and to have an impact on the media with their side of the story. Here is how it works.

Know Exactly What Your Messages Are

Too often, executives and professionals who are less media-experienced agree to an interview or seek the attention of the media without the proper clarity about what their message is or how to communicate it in language a reporter will find compelling. Suzanne Bates, an award-winning television news anchor and reporter and the author of *Speak Like a CEO: Secrets for Commanding Attention and Getting Results,* put it like this: "Reporters want opinion . . . . They want to know what you really think . . . . So they want compelling opinion, they want colorful language; they want you to put your stake in the ground . . . . "

It sounds easy, but before you can put your stake in the ground, you have to know where you stand. You have to understand your objectives, goals, and key messages thoroughly.

"Essentially, you've got to really listen and respond to the reporter, and answer the question they're asking," Bates continues, "while at the same time keeping in mind your position, or message, so that you can bridge to the powerful compelling messages . . . . This begins with a lot of thought about what your messages are. You have to think things through. You have to know what your position is in order to give an effective interview to a reporter." Susan Tellem, CEO of the high-profile PR firm Tellem Worldwide, adds, "Remember that it is not a conversation with the reporters. It's an opportunity for you to communicate your company's message, and tell the audience what your company is all about."

At GuruMaker, when we work on message development with our clients, I always ask, "What is the one thing you absolutely want the public to 'get'?" In response, I'll get a list of a dozen or more things they want the public to know. Unfortunately, in today's lightning-speed sound-bite culture, there is barely enough time to get one major message across, let alone several. Therefore, we "package" that one message in the kind of language that resonates with reporters, shareholders, clients, and future customers. Then we make sure to repeat the gist of the message as often as possible for the duration of the interview.

Say, for instance, your company has gone on a spending spree, purchasing struggling businesses left and right or buying new equipment, production plants, or technology. As a result, you're facing criticism from the public and your shareholders. The public is mad because you're acting like a playground bully, driving smaller operations out of business, and your shareholders are worried that you're depleting cash reserves with the spending spree. Your message to the public—imbued with your executive poise—could be that your corporate expansion is creating hundreds or thousands of new jobs that more than offset the temporary hardship suffered by a few smaller business owners. If that's your message, stick to that one main point. Put it into as few powerful words as possible, and the message will be clear and crisp when you get a chance to face the public via the media. The message to your nervous shareholders, who have a perspective different from that of the general public, might be that the acquisition of smaller businesses and new technology will boost productivity and increase market share in the long run, providing for a healthy organization with longevity.

Similarly, if you're getting flak for closing offices and laying off workers, your message might be that your "cost-cutting measures" provide a boost of vitality to the rest of the organization and ensure continued employment for the majority of the workers. This restored financial vitality may lead to the rehiring of laid-off staff once organizational health has been restored. When the cameras start rolling, you can drive that message home, supporting it with every word you say and every nonverbal gesture you make.

Although these examples provide an oversimplified version of a communications strategy, they illustrate how a powerful message can be put in simple terms that can be remembered easily and reinforced with repetition for impact.

Sometimes amateur spokespeople think that an interview with a reporter is a friendly chat. This couldn't be farther from the truth. Reporters have a job to do, and they'll do it even if it means making you look bad. They have their own agenda, and so should you. Work on developing a strong message and then take every opportunity to get it across to your target audiences. This leads us to step 2.

Get Your Key Messages Across No Matter What It Takes

No matter what the situation is, it's imperative that you find a way to tell your side of the story.

Susan Tellem agrees: "No matter what my client has done . . . no matter what the media is reporting, we always suggest we write a statement that will give them some information, so they can quote the client in the press. And my feeling is that if you stonewall the press, or you don't offer some kind of statement, you won't get a balanced story." As Tellem affirmed, by not conveying any of your messages to the press, you're willingly giving up the opportunity for balanced media coverage. If the reporter doesn't hear your side of the story, he'll print only the other side. If the public doesn't hear your side of the story, it will believe only the other side. It's that simple.

Sara Spaulding, a PR expert with the Denver-based firm Webb Public Relations, has learned the importance of being open with the media. One of Spaulding's past clients, a nonprofit organization, experienced some financial problems and had to close a few branches, leading to staff layoffs. Realizing that the media might take a negative view of the story, Spaulding made sure to work effectively with the local media and keep communication channels open. To achieve this, she found a local reporter she could trust to provide balanced reporting and gave him a call, saying, "We'd love for you come in and interview the CEO and really get the firsthand information about the restructuring." The result? The local media and the community understood the story behind the layoffs. They realized that the nonprofit was making tough decisions but doing the best it could. All in all, it was a good outcome for the organization, which might have faced some nasty headlines if it hadn't made the effort to tell its side of the story.

What if the reporter isn't receptive to your perspective or your messages? In that case, see Chapter 12, which covers this situation extensively: how to respond to difficult questions, how to take control of an interview that's veering off course, and how to stay on message during hostile questioning. In the meantime, let's move on to step 3.

Understand and Accept That Once You Say Something, It's True

It's true in the eyes of the public, that is. This can be a valuable tool but also a dangerous weapon. You have the opportunity to get your message out there and shape the public's opinion in an irrevocable way, and that can be very positive. However, if you tell a half-truth or an outright lie, you may create a weapon with which your opponents will take you down later. With publicly broadcasted messages you can create precisely the perceptions you aim to form in the minds of your audience, or you can derail your best efforts by choosing the wrong words, delivery, and nonverbal messages. The bottom line is that by commenting to the media, you create a lasting record and participate in shaping the future of your company's public image. We'll discuss this in more detail later.

Gil Bashe, executive vice president of the PR firm Makovsky & Company, explains the dangers: "Often when executives are speaking to the media, it's possible for them to feel like they are in the moment, when in fact they are speaking to the media. They are creating an indelible, enduring record of the company's position or progress on an issue." For example, Bashe says, if a health-care executive publicly makes a statement about the projected success of a certain initiative or medicine that affects large segments of society, people may decide to make investments on the basis of that information. If the pledge turns out not to be true, the company will have some angry shareholders. "What the executive says is always on the record . . . . They need to be conscious of what they're saying at any given time, and the effect it will have at that moment, and at moments to come."

Here is the strategy in a nutshell: Know your message and get it across, considering both the short-term and long-term effects of your words. It is a deceptively simple strategy that's used by the best communications experts because of the fact that it is highly effective when one is dealing with the media. In the next section, we'll go a little more deeply into how the media influence public opinion and how you can use their tactics and methodology for your organization and your personal agenda.

Spin: Why There Is No Such Thing as Unbiased Communication and What This Means to You

The Rise of Spin

Fairly or not, the concept of spin often is conflated with the entire field of public relations. Any business executive looking to manage public perception and raise his or her profile would do well to understand some of its illustrious history. Edward Bernays, generally considered the father of public relations, also was labeled "the father of spin" by his biographer Larry Tye. One of Bernays's first PR clients was the U.S. government; another was the tobacco industry. In 1929, Bernays helped the tobacco industry increase its appeal to women by orchestrating a famous PR stunt: putting cigarettes in the hands of feminists marching through the streets of New York. This encouraged women to see smoking as an important way to claim their rights.

The term *spin* first came into general use in the 1980s, when the media labeled PR experts with the pejorative name *spin doctors*. This use of the word *spin* was derived from sports such as baseball, in which a player puts a spin on the ball to trick another player.

Today, the word maintains connotations of deceit and trickery. Sometimes that's fair, and sometimes it's not. In this section, we put a new spin on spin and explain why it is probably the most ubiquitous phenomenon in human communication. In many cases, it's just another word for what most people do every day: tell a story from their own perspective.

There's No Such Thing as a No-Spin Zone

Maybe you've seen the conservative Fox News pundit Bill O'Reilly, who, for a long time, has claimed that his show is a no-spin zone. Although this may be an effective way to market his show, it is a fallacy. It's also false advertising. Why? Because there's no such thing as a no-spin zone.

At the most basic level, spin is a biased portrayal of a situation, a portrayal that matches one's own interpretation of events. However, there's no such thing as objective communication. There's no such thing as someone speaking without bias. Whenever anyone speaks—including you and I—his or her personal perspective affects what he or she says. It affects how we construct our sentences, what words we choose, which details we find important, and which details we don't. Not only that, it affects whether we discuss the topic at all. Choosing one topic to speak about but not another inherently conveys bias.

Nowhere is this demonstrated more effectively than in the media, which have tremendous communicative power and reach. The media do not have to go out of their way to spin things, although they do that on a regular basis. The personal biases and perspectives of those who create and edit broadcasts are their own form of spin.

There are multitudes of ways the media can influence public perception. Rising executives who want to influence the way others see them should take note of the media's strategies and apply them to their own situations.

Here are just a few of those strategies.

They Choose the Topic of the Message or the Broadcast. It seems obvious, but public opinion is shaped very heavily by whether the media choose to run a story at all. A great example is public perception of global warming. A few years ago, global warming almost never was featured or discussed on mainstream media outlets such as CNN. Today, there are stories about global warming on a regular basis. In reality, the scientific consensus on global warming has changed very little in the last few years; environmental scientists were just as clear about their perceptions of human-caused climate change in 2006 as they are today. However, the increased media attention paid to this subject has shaped public opinion, leading most people to believe that scientific consensus on global warming is a recent development.

They Create the Title of the Message. Even if the content of a news story or broadcast is neutral, an opinionated title can have a huge influence on the way the audience perceives and processes the content of the message. If the title is negative, the audience will construct the neutral facts it receives in a negative way. If the title is positive, it also influences the way the audience constructs the information. In fact, informal studies have shown that when two groups of people read the exact same article with different titles, they have markedly different readings.

They Determine the Timing of the Message.   Does the broadcast play during the six o'clock news, or is it relegated to a less popular hour? Does the story come out on a slow news day when it will be the headline, or does the news break on a particularly busy day, when it will pale in comparison to the "real" news? You may have heard the phrase "It's a good day to bury bad news." This phrase originated with the scandal concerning Jo Moore, a British political advisor. On September 11, 2001, after the attacks on the World Trade Center and the Pentagon, Moore infamously sent out an e-mail to her department's press office, stating, "It's now a very good day to get out anything we want to bury."

They Select Guests and Experts Who Share Perspectives.   The unlikeliest pair on TV split up long ago, but for the longest time when they lit up the screen together, media critics commented on the disparity between the two hosts on the former Fox News program *Hannity & Colmes*. Their promotional material used to say, "Conservative radio commentator Sean Hannity and liberal radio personality Alan Colmes offer their points of view in an often animated, always compelling debate." The catch was that Hannity came off as the more handsome and animated of the two (he was also the show's executive producer), whereas Colmes had a less appealing personality and by all accounts looks that only a mother could love. That disparity undoubtedly influenced and biased viewers' perceptions of the debate.

Another example is the frequent media practice of hosting "balanced" debates or panel discussions in which two guests come on the show to represent opposite opinions. This is a balanced debate in that both sides of the story get told, but there may not really be two sides to the story. Maybe the first guest is representing an opinion held by 95 percent of the professionals in the field and the second guest's colleagues widely consider him a nut job. Or maybe there are many more sides to the story than two and most opinions fall in the middle, whereas the two debaters hack away at straw men. When the media get to choose which guests appear, they're able to frame the argument for public debate in a way that may not reflect reality.

They Edit the Footage, Image Content, and Quotes and May Omit Whatever They Choose.   In the 1998 hit comedy *You've Got Mail,*

CEO Joe Fox (Tom Hanks) learns this lesson the hard way. Fox, the CEO of the big bad new bookstore in town, is getting a hard time from the media. In response, he delivers a five-minute speech to reporters, expounding on the appeal of cheap books, good coffee, and a friendly atmosphere. When the segment airs later that evening, Fox is unpleasantly surprised to find that they've edited his comments down to a 10-second clip in which he says: "I sell cheap books, sue me!" When Fox recovers, his business partner demands, "That's what you said?" Fox answers, "That's not all I said. I can't believe those bastards!"

Believe it. A biased or hostile reporter or editor can turn anything you say against you by taking it out of context, editing it, or controlling the length and framing of the broadcast. Of course, if Fox had been better trained in speaking to the media, he probably would have been able to avoid the unfavorable perception that was created of him. (For more information about crafting good quotable messages and speaking effectively to hostile media, see Chapter 12.)

They Determine the Camera Angles, the Close-Ups, and Sometimes the Background.   Where the camera lingers has tremendous influence on where the viewers' sympathies lie. Camera close-ups on an individual tend to generate viewer sympathy and rapport with that individual. Along slightly different lines, camera shots can be used to imply unsubstantiated connections. A reporter might make a statement while the camera pans in on a certain person. This enables the show to imply context without explicitly making accusations.

In another example, a show may choose a more flattering or less flattering angle from which to film a political speaker, depending on where its sympathies lie. The way the viewers see the speaker's message is highly dependent on how they see the speaker.

They Have the Ability to Encourage or Discourage Applause from the Studio Audience.   Political conventions are a perfect example. At those highly publicized political meetings, the audience is chosen carefully so that every sound bite the candidate utters will be greeted with enthusiastic applause. This sends an important message to the wider public audience about how they should interpret and process the candidate's words. The same goes for talk shows with studio audiences. Electronic signs or staffers with cue cards flash the word *applause* to a compliant audience, and the viewer at home perceives consensus.

As long as you continue to speak to the media, you will be subjected to these practices. The good news is that once you understand these common spin tactics, you can start adjusting to them and take greater control of the message.

In his article "The Myth of the Rhetorical Situation," Towson University Distinguished Professor Richard Vatz explores the power of language and its ability to affect perception. This article was published in 1973 but is just as relevant and controversial today. Vatz wrote the article as a counterargument to another theoretician, Lloyd Bitzer, who had published an article that argued that events and reality unambiguously dictate meaning, from which language and interpretations automatically follow. In other words, meaning is inherent in reality. Whatever is said about reality merely describes that meaning.

You might think this is obvious, but Vatz argues that it's not so straightforward. According to Vatz, meaning is not inherent in events. Language does not reflect an objective "reality" accurately. Instead, language *creates* reality. The world is complex, bewildering, and largely abstract. Language takes these abstractions and turns them into concrete concepts. In a very real way, language leads to reality, not the other way around.

As Vatz points out, very few of the situations we experience directly influence our own observable reality. Although we encounter certain events through personal observation—such as hunger, cold, and rain—for the most part "we learn of facts and events through someone's communicating them to us." Thus, the people who describe the events not only shape how we perceive those events, they decide whether we perceive them at all. This is significant, because, as Vatz says, "the world is a scene of inexhaustible events which all compete to impinge on . . . our sliver of reality." This is where spin comes into play.

Business executives on their way up should embrace the fact that there are dozens of ways to phrase a title. There also are dozens of angles from which to film a speaker and dozens of ways to edit a quotation. There are dozens of potential spokespeople to represent a single issue; some of those spokespersons are strong, and some are weak. As Vatz puts it, "One never runs out of context. One never runs out of facts to describe a situation."

Quite simply, spin is the art of finding the context and the facts that support one's telling of the story. Vatz states that every "communicator is involved in this sifting and choosing, whether it be the newspaper editor choosing front-page stories versus comic-page stories or the speaker highlighting facts about a person in a eulogy."

In fact, the eulogy situation is a great example. Every single one of us has done good things in our lifetimes as well as deeds we're not proud of. We've had shining moments, embarrassing moments, and regrettable moments. A kind eulogizer usually interprets this overwhelming mass of information in a way that is favorable to the individual, but imagine how a hostile eulogizer might interpret the same life. Most of us certainly have made enough mistakes in our lives to fill up a 15-minute speech.

This phenomenon will be demonstrated with even more clarity in the exercise at the end of this chapter. In the meantime, there is a great deal to learn from one of today's most esteemed spin doctors, the communications expert Frank Luntz, author of *Words That Work*. Luntz is a pollster who for a number of years tapped into people's emotions and reported back to his employer about its constituents' preferences and dislikes; his employer was one of the major political parties in the United States. His claim to fame is his assistance in crafting influential language that the conservative party in the United States used to manage the perceptions of voters. Detailed examples of some of his work are discussed below.

How to Frame Perceptions and Create Meaning with Words Alone

Ironically, the many biographies of Frank Luntz are themselves powerful indicators of the phenomenon of spin. Luntz's Web site states that he "is one of the most honored communications professionals in America today" and that "more media outlets have turned to Dr. Luntz to understand the hopes and fears of Americans than any other political pollster."

Critics take a dimmer view of Luntz, however, describing him as a "conservative elite persuader" attempting to "scrub our brains free of individual thoughts," a "right-wing spinmeister," and "a malevolent sleaze master we can learn from." Wikipedia weighs in somewhere in the

middle: "He is considered a master of the art of political propaganda."
Malevolent sleaze master or not, we can learn from him.

Here are some famous euphemisms attributed to Luntz:

- The "death tax" to refer to the estate tax
- "Climate change" as a less "heated" way to refer to global warming
- The "Clear Skies Initiative," referring to legislation that critics contend relaxes emissions regulations, making the skies a little *less* clear
- The "Healthy Forests Initiative" for legislation that promises, among other things, to move toward "removing needless administrative obstacles and providing authority to allow timber projects to proceed without delay when consistent with the Northwest Forest Plan"

Luntz is probably best known for his leaked memos. Throughout his tenure as communications advisor to the GOP, several of his memos have been leaked, offering the general public interesting insights into how an organization masters the art of staying on message. The most widely discussed of these memos dwelled on language about environmental policy. However, since this memo has been reported on in a number of places, I'm going to focus instead on a less-well-known memo attributed to Luntz that deals with language used to describe the war in Iraq. Parts from the leaked memo were reported on in the *Washington Post* in June 2004, and the full text can be found in several sites on the Internet. Below are several excerpts, with my commentary. The emphasis is in the original text.

The memo:

> *The overwhelming amount of language in this document is intended to create a lexicon for explaining the policy of "preemption" and the "War in Iraq."*
>
> *However, you will not find any instance in which we suggest that you use the actual world "preemption" or the phrase "the war in Iraq" to communicate your policies to the American public. To do so is to undermine your message from the start.*

"Preemption" may be the right policy, and "Iraq" the right place to start. But those are not the right words to use.

Your efforts are about "the principles of prevention and protection" in the greater "War on Terror."'

This is a clear-cut case of using a powerful euphemism. The phrase "prevention and protection" ostensibly means the same thing as the phrase "preemptive action," but the first phrase has a much more emotionally positive connotation. The conflation of "the War in Iraq" with the "War on Terror" is an example of an infamous tool of spin: relying on unproven assumptions as if they were truth. In fact, there were no meaningful connections between Iraq and al-Qaeda (or the attacks of 9/11), but this was not proved until later.

> <u>*Set the context: 9/11 changed everything.*</u> *On this issue more than any, context is everything. The American people have notoriously short attention spans—and they do not always see the big picture unless it is unveiled to them. Start with what we all hold in common—the shared experience of the tragedy on September 11th, but then explain what it has done to the present and what it means for the future.*

"Set the context" is an interesting choice of words here. As we learned earlier from Richard Vatz, "One never runs out of context." By choosing the tragic events of 9/11 as the context—and not, for instance, the relative safety experienced by the other 99 percent of Americans—the administration was able to shape and influence the tone of the conversation.

> <u>*Connect the dots. You have to explain Iraq's role in the "Wider War on Terror."*</u> *Americans expected smoking-gun caliber evidence of weapons of mass destruction. So long as that kind of irrefutable proof isn't available, a different tact toward indicting the Saddam regime must be taken. The Iraqi regime must be indicted because they committed <u>same kinds of actions as those of other terrorists.</u> Associate them by their actions, their goals, and their behavior.*

Here Luntz acknowledges a weakness in the party's PR strategy: the lack of evidence for any weapons of mass destruction. He also suggests a way to counter that weakness, rendering it obsolete. Take special note of this technique. Any executive planning to speak to the media should be well aware of any weaknesses in her or his organization and have a similar method ready with which to discount or direct attention away from that weakness.

> **_Once Iraq is established as part of the wider War on Terror, a greater case can be made for waging war THERE, not here._** *If you describe it simply as "pre-emptive action" some Americans will carry deep reservations about the rightness of the cause. Americans are conditioned to think that hitting first is usually wrong. If, however, you have successfully connected Iraq to the wider War on Terror, and if you are able to personalize this policy ("attacking them before they can attack us"), then you will have addressed their concerns.*

An appeal to fear is one of the most common types of propaganda, particularly political propaganda. As Luntz's promotional material states, he understands the "hopes and fears" of average Americans extraordinarily well. In this case, he explains how government officials can exploit Americans' fears, persuading them to circumvent their moral reservations and support something they'd normally view as wrong. Fear is one of the two most powerful motivators, and Luntz taps into it effectively.

This fascinating memo closely mirrors the administration's talking points in early 2004 and thus conveys another important message about spin. When used deliberately, spin is a powerful double-edged sword. It can work very well, as demonstrated by the wide public support for the war in Iraq during this period, but it also can backfire. Eventually, the public may begin to sense a disconnection between your words and your actions. They may even begin to feel that they've been deceived, and then they'll be angry. The result is a tidal wave of backlash.

A Discussion of Ethics

We've discussed the double-edged sword of spin: fortune for some, disaster for others. Business executives and professionals who make use of this critical influencing tool in creating their executive presence must know that success depends on how effectively this sword is wielded. Even the most masterful spinners must consider their audience. Ineffective spinning is telling your audience what *you* want them to hear. Effective spinning, as explained by Frank Luntz, is telling your audience what *they* want to hear. However, there are also ethical considerations.

Richard Vatz examined the ethical considerations in the article we discussed earlier in this chapter. As Vatz explains, the way you view the relationship between language and reality has a significant influence on your ethical decisions. If you acknowledge that language has the power to create meaning and represent reality in people's minds, you must accept responsibility for the way your words influence people's actions. Powerful companies, organizations, and politicians have tremendous power to shape public opinion and thus public action. That power comes with moral responsibility.

In this chapter, you've learned powerful secrets about couching your message in language that will connect with your audience and ways to shape and transform your executive image. You'll get some hands-on experience in the exercise I've included for you below. A word of caution: Choose to use these strategies only after careful consideration of your ethical boundaries and responsibilities.

Practicing the Art of Spin

For this part of the chapter, I'd like you to try one of my favorite exercises in persuasive language, an assignment I learned about from Vatz, who has been assigning this project to his students for over 30 years. I'd like you to try it now, keeping in mind everything we've learned about the power of spin, the flexibility of language, and the inherent bias in all forms of communication.

First, choose an opinion article in the popular press, such as a book review, a movie review, a music review, a restaurant review, or something else along those lines. Then rewrite the article from a different perspective, reversing the essence of its position. Here are the rules:

You may not change the facts of the article. You may only reverse the subjective opinions of the article. For example, if the original review says a long-running movie "seemed to drag on forever," you cannot say that the movie was short. However, you can say, "Even at two and a half hours, the movie easily managed to hold my attention."

The changes must be relevant to the material of the review. For example, in changing a positive restaurant review to a negative review, it would not be relevant to add that you were allergic to one of the dishes you tasted.

The changes must be plausible, reasonable, and substantial. Don't just add the word *not* to make an affirmative sentence negative. The goal here is to think like a newsmaker. The best revised articles will be the ones you easily can imagine picking up and reading, probably in the same place where you found the original article.

The viewpoint must be consistent. If a negative original concedes a positive point, in your rewrite the same point must be made even more positive. For example, if the original movie review says, "The only bright spot was a workmanlike performance on the part of so-and-so," the revised review should take it up a notch with something like "One of the most inspiring parts of the film was so-and-so's masterful performance."

Quotations can be eliminated or truncated. However, the intended meaning may not be subverted or the words changed. That is, if you choose an article that already has a positive or negative quotation in it, you cannot change the words of the speaker. However, as we saw earlier in this chapter, trimming the quotation may alter the speaker's intended meaning vastly. For example, if a speaker is quoted as saying that a particular restaurant "falls flat occasionally but overall offers an excellent dining experience," it would be acceptable to trim this quote down to the much more negative part of the quote ("falls flat").

Try it on the articles below. They're four examples that were chosen by Vatz's students at Towson University. Their interpretations of the assignments will be revealed later in the chapter, but resist the temptation to cheat by skipping ahead. Instead, explore and try out your new skills by following the directions above.

Example 1: Roberta Smith, "Tate Modern's Rightness versus MoMA's Wrongs," *New York Times*, November 1, 2006, p. E1.

But Tate Modern appears to have worked out many of its kinks. It is using its limitations to its advantage and evolving into a people's palace that the art world can also love.

The lessons of Tate Modern challenge a lot of conventional wisdom, at least that expressed in many American museums these days. Most important, Tate Modern's huge building proves that being big is not the same as being corporate: it is possible to have a large institution feel personal to its visitors.

Tate Modern is an enormously user-friendly place, physically comfortable and hospitable, with inexpensive places to eat and frequent opportunities to sit. Snack bars, restrooms, elevators, escalators and stairways are all conveniently grouped together in the core of the building.

Example 2: Bianca Sienra, "Catch the Wave," *Baltimore Magazine*, October 2006, p. 219.

It was probably a bad idea to have filled up so quickly on breads and accompaniments. The endless tapas menu is full of items we really wanted to try. So we bravely forged on and ordered our second round. An excellent version of tortilla Espanola—that wonderful omelet of potatoes and onions universal in Spanish tapas bars—was velvety and fluffy and rich with butter. Stuffed piquillo peppers were bursting with goat cheese and duxelle, and lay in a tomato sauce that gave an acid boost to the sweet, savory peppers.

Example 3: Michael Sragow, "Eastwood's Cliché-Riddled 'Flags' Doesn't Rate a Salute," *Baltimore Sun*, October 20, 2006, p. 1C.

Meanwhile, as if the film weren't already out of Eastwood's directorial control (or, worse yet, in it), there's a third strand of action involving Bradley's son, James (Tom McCarthy), interviewing witnesses to his father's wartime experiences. For all his ersatz realism and toughness, Eastwood uses this ploy to invoke the nostalgia for "the Greatest Generation" that permeated pre-Sept. 11 culture—and may now come back stronger than ever in the wake of disillusionment over the war in Iraq.

Example 4: Rashod D. Ollison, " '20 Years Old'? C'mon, Janet, Act Your Age," *Baltimore Sun*, September 26, 2006, p. 1D.

Once you start seeing her splashed on magazine covers without much clothing, you know Janet Jackson is about to come back with a new project. In the past two months, she has posed topless on the cover of Vibe and in a black two-piece lingerie set on the front of King. The performer has been announcing her periodic returns in such a way for more than a decade now.

Now choose one or a couple of these passages and try your skills at a persuasive rewrite, following the rules outlined above. When you're done, compare your results with the rewrites below that were done by Vatz's students. The following attempts each received an A.

Example 1 Rewrite

But Tate Modern continues to be plagued by some of these kinks and has been forced to evolve into a largely pedestrian audience, with little support from the art community.

The failures of Tate Modern are ones that could have easily been avoided if the designers had investigated the conventions American museums hold dear. The titan feel of the building itself has eradicated all opportunity for a personal or intimate experience by museum-goers.

Tate Modern seems at times to have dumbed itself down for the rainy day museum visitors, emphasizing seating and inexpensive food over an awe-inspiring collection. Snack bars, elevators, and escalators are the main attractions, as they are prominently on display in the center of the facility.

Example 2 Rewrite

If one dares to go to this restaurant, it might be a good idea to fill up on the breads, because what comes after will quickly douse their appetite. While the tapas menu has a lot to offer, there were few items that seemed genuinely appealing. However, my guest and I bravely forged on and ordered the next course. The tortilla Espanola, a traditional omelet of potatoes and onions—a staple in Spanish tapas bars—was drowning in butter with such a creamy taste that it was hard to swallow. The stuffed piquillo peppers had way too much goat cheese and duxelle so that the tomato sauce it lay in tasted acidic, and the peppers gave way to a sweet taste that contradicted the theme of the platter.

Example 3 Rewrite

The film progresses quite well in Eastwood's more-than-capable hands, as he ably manages to show the audience a third strand of action involving Bradley's son, James (Tom McCarthy), interviewing witnesses to his father's wartime experiences. With an abundance of realism and toughness, Eastwood exquisitely uses this plot line to bring us back to the nostalgia for "the Greatest Generation" that rightfully dominated 9/11 culture and may return as the United States bravely fights the war on terrorism and the war against nuclear proliferation on a multiplicity of new fronts, including Korea and Iran.

Example 4 Rewrite

Once you start seeing her illuminating magazine covers with her still striking figure, you know Janet Jackson is about to put out another great album. In the past two months she has enticed her audience, posing nearly au naturel on the cover of Vibe and electrifying the cover of King in black lingerie. For more than a decade, this pop idol has announced her long-awaited returns in this stimulating fashion.

If you want to flex your persuasive muscles a little more, try this exercise on a "hard news" article, rewriting it from a different perspective. This is a much more challenging task because these articles usually do not state an opinion; they're supposed to be as objective as possible. However, after close examination of a few news articles on the same topic, I think you'll begin to see how bias can operate even when no opinion is stated. Look for how the title is phrased, whose perspective the article seems to follow, which persons or entities are depicted as the subjects (conducting the major actions), and which persons or entities are depicted as the objects of those actions.

Work on developing your critical reading and persuasive writing skills with these exercises and you'll soon see your ability to influence others soaring beyond what you could have imagined.

In Chapter 12 we'll discuss some of these concepts and techniques in more detail. Like every spotlight moment, your moment in the media will require lots of planning, preparation, and rehearsal to be successful. I'll explain how to create compelling and lasting quotes, how to prepare for critical interviews, how to create the desired effect of a powerful executive presence through your appearance, and more.

12

How to Use the Media to Enhance Your Reputation and Raise Your Profile

It's a Sound Bite World: Crafting Quotes and Messages That Stand Out

"Silence is golden" may be an appropriate proverb at times, but not when you're receiving an award along with an opportunity to boost your visibility and profile.

Fashion designer Miuccia Prada, of the brand of that name, decided to stay mum upon receiving an award from the nonprofit Council for the United States and Italy. Accepting her award in the ballroom of the Plaza Hotel in New York, Prada dismissed the opportunity to anchor a brief message about her brand in the minds of the assembled high-profile audience. In explaining her silence, according to an AP reporter, Prada dissed the value of sound bites, saying: "I am not shy. I just don't like to be generic. I'm not able to speak in sound bites. So I don't do it."

Prada is hardly alone in the perception that sound bites are "generic," "superficial," and "simplistic" and somehow lack substance. Many executives fear that a lengthy speech or one-hour interview will be edited down to an eight-second sound bite that may tell a story different from what was intended, will be taken out of context, and will make a powerful statement on its own. Many times they're right; that is why executives and professionals who are keen to advance their business or their personal brand need to craft and rehearse sound bites that reflect their message accurately, are compelling to the media and the audience, and can be recalled easily. Accomplish this and your words are much less likely to be used out of context to create a meaning that is damaging to you or the organization.

Sound bites—well-thought-out intentional ones at least—are a communicator's best friend, as they get the message across in a pithy statement, catching people's attention and ringing in their ears long after the talking is done. Contrary to what its detractors say, a well-crafted and strategic sound bite gives the listener context as opposed to voiding it.

Here are some examples of sound bites from politics that will live on in the recorded media, instantly recalling the entire context of the message they carried:

- Patrick Henry to Virginia delegates in 1775: "Give me liberty or give me death."
- Ronald Reagan at the Brandenburg Gate in Germany: "Mr. Gorbachev, tear down this wall."
- Ronald Reagan in a 1984 reelection campaign debate with younger opponent Walter Mondale: "I will not make age an issue in this campaign. I am not going to exploit, for political purposes, my opponent's youth and inexperience."
- George H. W. Bush at the 1988 Republican convention: "Read my lips, no new taxes."
- Vice-presidential candidate Lloyd Bentsen to opponent Dan Quayle in a 1988 televised debate: "Senator, I served with Jack Kennedy. I knew Jack Kennedy. Jack Kennedy was a friend of mine. Senator, you're no Jack Kennedy."
- President Bill Clinton in a videotaped deposition to prosecutors in the Monica Lewinsky affair: "It depends on what the meaning of the word 'is' is."

- Senator Barack Obama to Senator Hillary Clinton in a 2008 presidential campaign debate regarding her vote on the Iraq war: "It's not just saying you're ready for Day One. The question is, are you right on Day One?"
- Senator Hillary Clinton during a debate in the 2008 presidential campaign: "It did take a Clinton to clean up after the first Bush, and it might take another one to clean up after the second one."
- President Barack Obama in a speech to House Democrats in the first month of his administration, pushing to get the stimulus bill passed: "We can't afford to make perfect the enemy of the absolutely necessary."

Of course sound bites are dropped everywhere, not just in politics. Consider Johnnie Cochran's unforgettable sound bite during O. J. Simpson's murder trial, speaking about a bloodied glove Simpson allegedly wore: "If it doesn't fit, you must acquit." We all know how that ended.

Sound bites not only capture the essence of an argument for those who hear them; they often carry an emotional wallop too. That's why persuasive communication often is supported by sound bites.

Consider this sound bite by Steve Jobs, made as a comment to Pepsi's John Sculley in persuading him to become Apple's CEO:

Do you want to spend the rest of your life selling sugared water or do you want a chance to change the world?

Then there was the one Jobs made during a commencement address at Stanford University in 2005:

Remembering that I'll be dead soon is the most important tool I've ever encountered to help me make the big choices in life. Because almost everything—all external expectations, all pride, all fear of embarrassment or failure—these things just fall away in the face of death, leaving only what is truly important. Remembering that you are going to die is the best way I know to avoid the trap of thinking you have something to lose. You are already naked. There is no reason not to follow your heart.

Here is another quote from the sound-bite-savvy Apple founder that captures the essence of his creative genius: "Why join the Navy when you can be a pirate?"

An enduring sound bite by former General Electric CEO Jack Welch hinted at his mettle when he said about the various business units within GE: "We're either number one or number two, or we'll get out of the business."

Of course, certain sound bites—particularly those spoken carelessly without strategic purpose or without much thought given to their positive or negative impact before one utters them—can shape a public speaker's reputation in the minds of the listeners, forever associating the speaker with the message of an unfortunate sound bite.

Who doesn't remember the sound bite "Only the little people pay taxes," attributed to the late hotel magnate Leona Helmsley, dubbed the "Queen of Mean," who served prison time for tax evasion and tax fraud. That sound bite followed her around for the rest of her life, serving as her brand message wherever she went.

MSNBC's David Shuster got himself in hot water when he referred to Chelsea Clinton as being "pimped out" by her mother's campaign, a sound bite that prompted calls for him to be fired. The offending sound bite was wrapped in the following quote by Shuster: "But doesn't it seem like she's being—but doesn't it seem as if Chelsea is sort of being pimped out in some weird sort of way?"

Speaking as a surrogate for presidential contender John McCain in the 2008 campaign, former Hewlett-Packard CEO Carly Fiorina opined that "no one on either the Republican or Democratic Party's presidential ticket has the experience to run a major company like Hewlett-Packard," but "that's not what [they are] running for." My bet is that back at the campaign headquarters strategists were pulling their hair out after hearing that one.

Reputation- and career-damaging sound bites don't even have to contain words; vocal gaffes can handicap the source when a sound bite goes on a national media tour that includes both late-night talk shows and every large or small media outlet online and offline. As a result of relentless replays in the media, Howard Dean's scream during the 2004 primaries and Al Gore's audible sighs during debates with George W. Bush in 2000 became negative focal points that Dean and Gore couldn't shake and couldn't win with.

Comedian and political pundit Bill Maher had his own take on this: "I was watching Andrea Mitchell . . . talking about debates, and she said, 'A sighing Gore, a sweating Nixon, a seemingly bored Bush, those unfortunate unscripted moments that voters sometimes remember most.' And I thought, yeah, they remember most because you show it on a loop on your media twenty-four hours a friggin' day! That's why they remember it most! It's not the voters who [choose]. It's what the media pick. The media picks out a few moments and they show it over and over again. And then people go, 'Well, Gore sighed; he's toast.'"

Even if you're not in the public eye, sound bites are every bit as important whether they occur in crucial conversations in which you want to have an impact, job interviews, or speeches. The common denominator here is that you want to be memorable. You want the core of your message, your argument, to be remembered.

How do you do that? How do you come up with nuggets that create an audience response and that are remembered and captured by any attendant media?

- *Know who's listening*: You have a reason for talking—one hopes—and your audience has a reason for listening to you. Otherwise they would switch channels or decline your invitation. If you're the boss and they have to listen to you, you especially want to make sure to insert sound bites so that even the unmotivated capture the essence of what you're saying. Write down the possible reasons people are listening to you and not someone else. What do they stand to gain or lose from your message? What are their needs and objectives? What would they care about that you're going to say?
- *Make it personal*: When you know what your audience expects from you, you can shape your message from their perspective. Whatever is on their minds, your sound bites have to answer that question, solve that problem, give them hope, teach them something, or tell them something they didn't know.

- *Edit ruthlessly*: Now that you have created a message from the audience members' perspective that's important to them, you have to break the message down into only the most compelling, most important parts. Strip away everything that is not absolutely necessary for understanding.

- *Shape what's left*: You're looking for stickiness, so keep in mind that key components of powerful sound bites are simple words, brief sentences void of jargon. They must be 100 percent relevant to the overall message you're conveying. To make them memorable, use rhetorical devices such as repetition, antithesis, contrast, shock, rhyme, and alliteration. This will give your statements salience and rhythm and differentiate them from the boilerplate stuff people hear and quickly tune out. Borrow liberally from commercials, the news, and famous quotes and rearrange or change those words slightly to fit your message. Piggyback on established frames and your message will benefit from the groundwork others have laid. A famous Wendy's commercial was based on the phrase "Where's the beef?" Countless politicians used the phrase in their messages to make them stand out when they were speaking of something that was lacking in substance. There are literally thousands of sound bites like this that the media have promoted and that have anchored themselves in people's brains. Make use of them to anchor your own message.

- *Test it*: People are always trying to make sense of what they hear and perceive. Since we're all up to our eyeballs in information, we want the executive summary, the nuggets, the truffles, the essence. With your sound bites you're helping people get it. You're making it easy for them. To test how easy, rehearse your message and the integrated sound bites with formal or informal focus groups and see what they pick out. Then adjust the message accordingly.

Reporters don't want to repeat word for word what you've said, and so they'll look for the truffles in your message. The more you create those truffles within your message, the more they'll end up in the minds and stories of the audience.

Mastering the Art of Q&A: Ten Techniques for Responding to Difficult Questions and Enhancing Your Credibility

We've all drawn a blank on occasion, forgetting names, numbers, places, or a story we wanted to tell. When it happens to our older compatriots, we call it having a senior moment. When it happened to the governor of South Carolina in an interview with CNN's Wolf Blitzer, people in the blogosphere called it embarrassing. It was a Sunday morning in 2008 at a time when no one outside Alaska had ever heard of Sarah Palin, and the South Carolina conservative Mark Sanborn was a hot contender for McCain's post of second in command. That was until Wolf Blitzer asked Sanborn a question on CNN live that probably ended Sanborn's candidacy for the VP pick, long before his affair with an Argentinean mistress came to light in 2009.

Here's the question Blitzer asked:

> *Are there any significant economic differences between what the Bush administration has put forward over these many years as opposed to now what John McCain supports?*

And here is Sanborn's fateful answer:

> *Um, yeah. For instance, take, you know, take, for instance, the issue of—I'm drawing a blank, and I hate it when I do that, particularly on television.*

He went on, still not saving himself:

> *Take, for instance the contrast on NAFTA. I mean, I think that the bigger issue is credibility in where one is coming from, are they consistent where they come from.*

Shortly thereafter, top blogs such as Huffingtonpost.com and media outlets such as CNN kept focusing on Sanborn's inability to think on his feet, dubbing him "the next Dan Quayle." A YouTube video of his gaffe quickly garnered over 20,000 hits. It was game over for the governor, who generally was considered a very able and smart politician.

Although Wolf Blitzer's question wasn't exactly a trick question, it was one that should have been anticipated in light of the context of the interview as well as an issue that was brought front and center for the Republican campaign early on.

To avoid a similar fate if you have the opportunity to bolster your image on national TV and enhance your reputation, here are my top 10 techniques for responding to difficult questions and enhancing your credibility:

1. Anticipate

As in the example above, a lack of focused preparation and anticipation of questions, attacks, rhetorical curveballs, and easily produced facts can make an interviewee look like Dan Quayle. Quayle earned this distinction and learned this lesson in debating Lloyd Bentsen in 1988 when he had no comeback for Bentsen's famously devastating attack (see the quote above) on Dan Quayle's self-comparison to John F. Kennedy. Even as vice president, the incident followed Quayle around and lodged itself firmly in the playbook of political gaffes that could have been avoided. The moral of the story is this: Whatever you hope the media won't ask about, they will. Whatever you think is long forgotten, isn't. Whenever you think you can just wing it, think again. Prepare for any questions you could be asked, including the worst and least anticipated (those especially), and have an answer that makes sense and won't define your interview and you for the rest of archived history.

2. Bridge It

As we said before, a reporter's objective is often to get a story that you don't want to tell, and so reporters will ask questions you don't want to answer. The solution in this case is to "bridge" from the question you don't want to answer to the message you want to get across. Be careful, though; this is not the time to be the proverbial bull in the china shop or pull a Stonewall Jackson. This is where nuance and dexterity come in. Reporters are smart people and will know when you're blatantly trying to avoid a question. However, if you do it subtly, you can outwit even Wolf Blitzer.

There are two types of questions reporters are particularly fond of: First, there's the "what if" question that is supposed to elicit speculative information from the interviewee to get to the truth, as the interviewee's likely answer presumably will reside somewhere near what's really going on so that the interviewee will avoid contradicting himself or herself in the media. A good bridge for a what if question that inherently focuses on the future would be to say, "We can speculate endlessly about what might be, but it's more important that we look at what's happening now and what we're doing about that. For instance . . . ."

The other type of question reporters like to ask is the "gotcha" question. These questions often start with "Previously you stated that . . . " or "You were quoted in the past as saying . . . " or "Your company put out a statement that mentioned . . . ."

To avoid being tied down during the interview by a statement you made that has nothing to do with the message you are trying to send now, a good bridge might be "You're absolutely right, and what we need to focus on now . . . " or "You've obviously done your homework, but so have we. Under the current conditions we have to look at . . . ."

Other bridging statements to your key message can include the following:

- "And what's also important to consider is . . ."
- "And to put it in proper context we have to look at . . ."
- "And let's not forget . . ."
- "What this relates to in the bigger scheme of things . . ."
- "As I've said before . . ."
- "Having said that . . ."
- "And it's important to look at the flip side . . ."
- "Let me put what you're saying in perspective . . ."
- "And we can add the fact that . . ."
- "And upon closer scrutiny we see . . ."
- "There is clearly room to argue that we . . ."
- "Speaking from my unique perspective, I can say . . ."
- "What's left out here is the issue of . . ."

- "That's a misconception, and the real question should be . . ."
- "To clarify . . ."
- "This reminds me of a similar situation . . ."
- "To answer, let me rephrase what I said earlier . . ."
- "And there's clearly room for improvement, which is why . . ."
- "In looking back, I can say . . ."
- "What your sources didn't mention . . ."
- "In the interest of fairness . . ."

3. Get the Facts

You may be asked a question to which you don't have a good answer and for which all the anticipation in the world wouldn't have prepared you. In that case simply and honestly say, "I do not have the facts on this, so I can't answer your question" or "Let me look into this and I promise I'll get back to you with an answer." If the reporter insists that the facts are widely known, say, "I'm sure you have reliable sources, but I would like to conduct my own research into this." A simple and straightforward "I don't know" may suffice, but make sure that it's okay not to know the answer. The last thing you want to do is look ignorant in the media.

4. Check the Premise

Reporters will sneakily insert a premise that, if you accept it, will frame you in a way you don't want. Here's a typical question: "Why aren't you concerned that the thousands who've been laid off from your company are still waiting for unpaid overtime?" Make sure the reporter's premise is correct. For instance, in referring to "thousands," the reporter may be including old data, when in fact many of those laid off were relocated or rehired, or she may be referring to layoffs that pertain to a merger in which laid-off workers received generous severance packages, or perhaps instead of overtime pay the company decided to continue paying health insurance for the workers for a specified amount of time. Plus, who said you're not concerned? Before you accept the premise of a question, check it carefully and answer the hidden charges within the question first. Reporters often, but not always, get it right.

5. Ask a Counterquestion

This can madden journalists but help you avoid hot water. For instance, the question "Why haven't you disclosed this information sooner?" may be answered as follows: "Why did you and the rest of the media feel it appropriate to report 'facts' when in fact you didn't have all of the facts on [insert the issue at hand here]?" Here's another option: "Would you find it responsible for us to go public with information we felt was incomplete?" Be careful with this strategy as it could inflame the exchange and spur the reporter to apply more intense pressure.

6. Frame It Your Way

Reporters and the media in general like to define the issue, ask the questions they want answered, and steer the discussion in a direction that serves them. That is why you need to introduce your own theme and take control of the discussion early on. If the reporter wants to make it about corporate greed, frame the discussion in terms of your commitment to fiscal responsibility—it's a flexible term—and the provision of shareholder value. If the reporter wants to define the interview in terms of your poor environmental record, mention your company's efforts—you'll have to prove that you have at least started in that direction, as in GE's self-reinvention from major polluter to green champion—to eliminate waste and advance a green agenda that will reduce the company's environmental footprint substantially. Above all, mean it or all the rhetorical gymnastics won't save you from a public tongue-lashing from the lips of Anderson Cooper et al.

7. Tell a Story

If you feel that an analogy, case study, or well-known story would be the best way to answer the question on your terms, use it. You can say: "In answer to your question, let me tell you a quick story." Make sure the story is relevant, appropriate, and not too long or you'll get interrupted. Pick the right story, and not only will it answer the question, it will help advance your agenda and hit your key message points at the same time.

8. Distinguish between Apples and Oranges

Reporters often compare a similar situation to yours to get a reaction from you. A typical question might be: "Wells Fargo has offered to give back the bailout funds they've received from the government and ultimately the taxpayers. Why haven't you?" Your answer: "Wells Fargo is in a completely different situation than we are, and obviously there are too many details where a simplistic comparison doesn't make sense." Then you can bridge back to your message, as was discussed above.

9. Tell the Truth

This is a novel concept in a litigious society in which everyone is afraid to accept responsibility for fear of being persecuted in the media and in court. However, the truth is underrated, and as we'll learn in Chapter 15, a genuine mea culpa not only can save one's reputation, it can boost it. If you've made a mistake, admit to it and explain how you will make up for it. If you're uncomfortable with this, check with your lawyers to consider any consequences. The bottom line is that transparency is not just a buzzword anymore. It's part of the rules by which the game is played.

10. Practice Emotional Detachment

Media archives and Internet video-sharing sites are full of footage of interviews that went off course, after which the interviewee suddenly ripped the earphones out or the lapel microphone off and stormed out of the studio. That's almost never a good idea as it suggests to the viewing audience that the reporter has hit a major nerve and that there is not just smoke but a full-blown fire that the interviewee is trying to hide. Listen carefully to the questions and respond with a friendly tone and an even temper. If you're all worked up from the interview, you can punch a pillow later or scream in the car with the music turned up, but never let people know that they got to you.

A Couple of No-Nos When Talking to the Media

Saying "No comment" to a reporter is like cutting oneself in shark-infested waters. Instead, tell reporters that you will give a full account of the situation as soon as you have all the facts and that you want to be absolutely accurate. This will buy you some time. It is even better if you can set a date by which you will speak on the issue.

Sometimes reporters and cable pundits get downright hostile when they feel they can't make headway with you. Don't take the bait. Remember hint 10: Stay cool and collected and remind the reporter that anger and manipulative pressure tactics don't resolve issues in the real world and won't resolve anything during the interview.

Remember that everything you say not only can and will not be held against you, it will be archived and available on the Internet until the earth crashes into the sun—maybe longer. Don't succumb to knee-jerk statements that come back to haunt you. Know the issues and speak intelligently and factually unless you want to end up as Jon Stewart's piñata on the *Daily Show* via a YouTube clip.

The Importance of Grooming and Outfits

Most people who plan to go to a party or a job interview think carefully about what they are going to wear. People check their fingernails, skin, and hair and make sure they don't have the remnants of a granola breakfast stuck in their teeth. You can multiply the need to do this by a million when you get exposure from the media.

People consider your judgment when they watch you and listen to you via the media. If you're Boy George, Vivienne Westwood, or Jean-Paul Gautier, face paint, large hats, and Scottish kilts are part of your self-presentation. If you are an executive who has a story to share about your organization or a political candidate who needs to influence constituents, you have to pay attention to the proper decorum. As a rule of thumb, consider the reaction you would get if you ran into your most important customer or any other person whose attitude and judgment matters to you. Then adjust accordingly.

Incidentally, the rules have changed somewhat, and you'll know when you can bend them to your preference and still project an executive presence with your clothes and accessories. If you're a British billionaire and CEO like Sir Alan Sugar or Virgin's Richard Branson, wearing the coat but losing the tie is cool and standard; it's called Continental style. If you're the twentysomething founder of Facebook, showing up in trademark flip-flops at a televised panel discussion is acceptable because it's "quirky." Steve Jobs's black turtlenecks and DirectTV CEO Chase Carey's handlebar mustache are considered trademarks that add to the aura and executive presence of those successful business leaders. Of course, top-ranked CEOs of billion-dollar companies and superrich business tycoons are 800-pound gorillas—doing what they please—whose unique dress codes and grooming habits are almost always interpreted as eccentric and interesting. This is something the lower pay scales among business executives may aspire to but should emulate only with extreme caution.

The point is that everything matters and everything is magnified when you're in the public eye. For the most part, people expect corporate executives to wear a suit and tie. Whether we think it is important or not is often beside the point. The public cares very much about these seemingly insignificant and personal aspects of self-presentation, and smart communicators heed their expectations.

Your clothing and grooming speak volumes. If nothing else, they say you respect your audience and pay attention to details. Even if you don't buy from the top-tier designers and manufacturers, make sure your suits are well tailored. Colors should match—shoes, belts, ties, accessories— and should be appropriate for the situation. Err on the side of being conservative if you're not sure and look rested and energetic when you face the media and your public. Otherwise, you may be sending a message that distracts people from what you really want to get across or even contradicts it.

In Chapter 13, we'll look at how you can use a number of media opportunities that are available to you—offering you a chance to assert your executive poise to key constituencies—and leverage them to spread your message among your audience.

13

Top Seven Secrets for Success
with the Media

IN THIS CHAPTER you will find everything you need to know about public relations and business success via the media.

Think of the media this way: The conversation already is happening, and you need to get into it. To be heard, you have to say or do something worthwhile that will get people's attention.

Whether you are at the top of the corporate flowchart or are eying the C-level from a distance—from a cubicle or a kitchen table—with aspirations to a corner office, knowing how to use the media effectively and leveraging any opportunities that present themselves or that you seek out on your own can be a key to business and personal success. How do you participate? What are the secrets to staying in the conversation?

Here are my top seven secrets to help you connect with customers, key stakeholders, and the general public as you aim for your share of minds and markets through the media

1. Accept the Invitation

If you are already at the C-level, you have a head start because people want to hear from you. According to research conducted by Burston Marseller, a global public relations and communications firm that tracks participation in executive forums among C-level executives, CEOs are flooded with invitations to speak at conferences, receiving an average of 175 requests a year. Most of these high-profile events are covered by industry and often national media, so carefully sift through the pile of invitations and decide which ones give you the biggest return on investment—the biggest bang for the buck. After all, you have a company to run.

2. Fashion Yourself as a Thought Leader

If you are an expert in your industry and can offer cutting-edge ideas, opinions, and angles no one else has thought about—or hasn't spoken up about—you are interesting to the media. It's what they look to cover in their efforts to bring news and trends to certain demographics. In cultivating your reputation as an expert, be careful to avoid jargon when talking to the media or you'll be interesting to only the few who don't mind wading through the lingo you've become accustomed to using in your line of expertise.

Demonstrate your passion; take a stand and tell stories—remember, the media loves them—that show how you or your business overcame challenges in the industry and what others can learn from your experiences. Use common sense, however, and be careful not to disclose any proprietary information that can land you in hot water with your corporate legal department or the board. Do talk about the future: what challenges are next and how one can best position oneself to make it through the storm. A healthy dose of optimism tagged on to a sober message will get you invited back. No one likes a doomsayer. If you think a healthy dose of fear is in order to wake people up and create an impact, don't forget to offer solutions. Fearmongering alone paralyzes, according to research. Add a solution and people will be more motivated to move in that direction.

3. Mind Your Message

We discussed the power of sound bites in Chapter 12. Nothing will get you quoted faster and with more certainty than a well-crafted sound bite that contains the core of your message or argument. Keep in mind, however, that the media love controversy and a good verbal faux pas, often delivered via an unintentional, not so strategic sound bite. Gaffes to the media don't come only in sound bites, however; sometimes they are packaged in a press release, a spokesperson's statement, a prepared speech, or a microphone that accidentally was left on. Although some of these messages certainly will get you in the news, it won't be in a way that is helpful to you or your organization. Here are a few examples that demonstrate this.

Robert J. Coury, CEO of Mylan Laboratories, one of the world's leading generic and specialty pharmaceutical companies, sent out a press release that predicted that Mylan would be safe from competition for at least seven months for a top product that had generated about 20 percent of the company's revenue in the previous quarter. That sounded like great news to shareholders. Until that afternoon, that is, when news broke that the Food and Drug Administration had just approved the marketing of another generic version of the name-brand drug; previously, only Mylan Laboratories had had the FDA's approval to market a generic version. The FDA's announcement directly contradicting CEO Coury's message to shareholders that morning sent the company's stock into a nosedive and called the CEO's judgment into question after a similarly damaging public statement he had made just a year earlier.

Alan Schwartz, the CEO of Bear Stearns, made some thoroughly misguided statements during an interview on CNBC on March 12, 2008, when he commented on the firm's stability: "Our liquidity and balance sheet are strong. . . . We don't see any pressure on our liquidity, let alone a liquidity crisis."

Less than two days later Bear Stearns in essence was declared bankrupt. Although the experts debate whether Schwartz intentionally misspoke or simply didn't see the train that was about to hit him, his executive presence evaporated with the CNBC interview that preceded—by just 36 hours—the precipitous fall of the global investment bank.

Then there's the former CEO of Lehman Brothers, Richard Fuld, who on an investor conference call on September 10, 2008, reassured the company's shareholders with this comment: "We are on the right track to put these last two quarters behind us." Lehman's CFO at the time, Ian Lowitt, said on the same call, "Our liquidity pool also remains strong at $42 billion." Whatever comfort investors felt after the conference call probably turned into disbelief and shell shock when Lehman Brothers filed for bankruptcy a mere five days later, reportedly the largest bankruptcy in history.

Be careful about what you say and where or to whom you say it. Any prepared or unprepared statements that don't pass muster or don't conform to facts and recorded history can leave a significant dent in your reputation. Unless you've built up a fairly sizable amount of goodwill before a messaging gaffe, it can sink your credibility and surface when you most need to inspire trust in your leadership.

4. Create a Stunt

The British business mogul and mediapreneur Richard Branson won't do without them. Knowing how much the media love a good stunt, Virgin Group founder Branson has garnered widespread media coverage and millions of dollars in free publicity in promoting the Virgin brand with everything from driving a tank down New York City's Fifth Avenue, to leaping off the Palms Hotel in Las Vegas, to crossing the Pacific in a hot-air balloon, breaking a record in the process. Branson says, "Using yourself to get out and talk about it is a lot cheaper and more effective than a lot of advertising. In fact, if you do it correctly, it can beat advertising hands down and save tens of millions of dollars." Of course, Branson is not the only CEO who knows how to get the attention of the media with unusual maneuvers.

Another great example—I referred to it earlier in Chapter 10—is Microsoft's chairman, Bill Gates, who was presenting at the prestigious TED (Technology, Entertainment, Design) conference in early 2009 and who made his point about malaria in developing countries. To underscore his points, he opened and unleashed a glass jar full of mosquitoes at the audience, telling them, "Not only poor people should experience the problem." The bugs reportedly were few and none carried the malaria virus, of course, but his point was made, and the ensuing media attention brought more publicity to one of Gates's pet issues than would have been achieved if he had just made the point verbally in his presentation.

5. Write Something Worthwhile

A book. A white paper. A research study that revolutionizes what people know about your industry or any industry. This point tags on to the section above on becoming a thought leader. Although being an expert is a good start, your expertise needs to be documented. That's what builds a path of respect for your opinion, your research, and your perspective in general. Write important things that people want to read and your reputation and executive presence will grow. People will talk about you, discuss your ideas in schools, and follow your lead in thinking about stuff differently.

You can be a contrarian, even controversial. You can say up when others say down, left when they say right. Take an accepted point of view and turn it on its head but be sure you can explain why. You have to have good reasons. Otherwise, you'll get laughed out of town. However, they laughed at Christopher Columbus too, so start thinking, probing, and writing. If you can't do it yourself, hire a good researcher and a ghostwriter and set sail toward the other side of public opinion and common knowledge. You may find that you come back with the new *Good to Great, The Four-Hour Work Week,* or *Outliers.* Watch the media frenzy ensue.

6. Put Your Name on Something

If you have the spare change, consider putting your name on a major sports center or arena, which can cost between $3 million and $10 million per year, with contracts up to 30 years. Big banks as well as investment and financial groups have a lock on this type of publicity, as do corporations such as Compaq and American Airlines. Having a law school named after you is not much cheaper, according to a study by the law professor Robert Jarvis of Nova Southeastern University. The price of legacy, as it was referred to in the *National Law Journal*, is anywhere between $3 million for Nova, Jarvis's employer, which was named in 1989, to an asking price of $100 million for the University of Minnesota Law School in 2007. Deeper pockets are needed to have a medical school adorned with your moniker. For the UCLA David Geffen School of Medicine, the movie mogul paid a handsome $200 million in 2002. Of course, there are more affordable ways to get media coverage and have your name on the tips of tongues and in the forefronts of minds.

You could discover an asteroid or a new insect species or create a new type font that Apple or Microsoft just has to have. All could bear your name, in Latin in the case of the insect species. More realistically, however, you could name an award, a charity you started, a scholarship you could give out every year, or an annual event you sponsor. Imagine inviting the media to cover the annual Winston Capital (that's you) Downhill Ski Racing Cup in Aspen or getting media attention in announcing the winners of the Mehmet Kazgan (you again) Computer Science Scholarships, in which a number of students get financial help from you or your organization to acquire critical computer skills. Be creative and promote it on your Web site, online postings, and print collateral to let the media see it's not just a gimmick but a real effort to bring value to a group of people. The bigger the event is and the more people who are affected, the more likely it is that you'll be covered by the reporters whose beat you're on.

7. Ride the Wave

As was mentioned at the beginning of this chapter, the conversation already is happening. Whether you have your first cup of coffee by logging on to Bloomberg, drudgereport.com, or technewsworld.com or flip through the *National Review* on the train as you head for the office, you'll see that there's a conversation happening right now that you can get in on. See what's on everyone's mind right now. Is it rising unemployment? An increase in corporate fraud at the senior executive level? A soaring—or tumbling—Dow Jones? The trade deficit? China's economy? Whatever it is, you can ride the buzz wave if you have something valuable to contribute to the conversation. The hard part is choosing which wave to get on. When you read about a child-obsessed mother who has octuplets, adding to her six children already at home, what angle of commentary or expertise can you offer if you're a fertility doctor, a child welfare advocate, or a psychologist? As a financial expert, when you see Suze Orman on CNN giving financial advice to people who were living from paycheck to paycheck and are now without a paycheck, can you offer valuable expertise right now that is more targeted to the masses who are destitute versus Orman's often criticized narrow approach?

Be specific and aggressive in getting in on the conversation. Here again, social media have a low barrier to entry (if you can type), but the momentum of your message can carry you onto the major networks if you're spot-on, timely, and good at what you do.

The seven secrets I just shared with you on how to engage the media are your starting point. With creativity and a burning desire to share your message, you'll discover other ways to have an impact on your target market and establish a powerful presence via the media.

In Chapter 14 you'll learn how in this era of transparency and technology your reputation is linked to Google and the other search engines and what you can do to avoid sabotaging the public perceptions you've worked hard to create.

PART V

REPUTATION MANAGEMENT: YOUR GOOD NAME IS ALL YOU HAVE

14

You've Been Googled:
What's the Verdict?

"CONSUMERS ARE MOVING their lives online," said Google CEO Eric Schmidt in a recent interview with *Fortune* magazine. To put the Google chief's statement into perspective, consider the bizarre story of Hasan Elahi and a life "gone online."

Elahi, a Bangladesh-born U.S. citizen and a professor at Rutgers University, had an unexpected run-in with the FBI in 2002 just after returning from a trip to the Netherlands. He was arrested and detained at the airport in Detroit before learning that he'd been placed on an FBI terrorist watch list after someone sent a tip to the feds alleging that he was stashing explosives somewhere in Florida. Although Elahi was cleared in the subsequent investigation, he was worried that this might happen again and that the next time he might be sent to at Guantánamo as an enemy combatant before he was cleared again.

Not wanting to take the chance, Professor Elahi took transparency to the extreme and started posting his entire life—moment by moment—online, leading *Wired* magazine to call him "the Visible Man."

Elahi figured that to keep the government off his back and neutralize further inquiries into a travel schedule that has him jetting around the world to conferences and art exhibits, he would turn his life into a real-life version of the Jim Carrey movie *The Truman Show*. He started a Web site called trackingtransience.net, onto which he constantly uploads snapshots of his surroundings. Among the tens of thousands of images of airports he's in, meals he consumes — on planes and on the ground — restrooms he uses, highways he travels on, and coffee shops he sits in, the professor can be tracked in real time via a GPS device he carries with him at all times. This way, he figures, the FBI or Homeland Security can log on and watch him by satellite shopping at a Safeway in San Francisco, sipping an Americano at a Starbucks in midtown Manhattan, or snacking on peanuts aboard a United flight across the ocean. According to *Wired*, which interviewed the professor, his server logs show hits from a number of government agencies, including the Pentagon and the Office of the Secretary of Defense.

So far Elahi's technotransparency has kept him in the clear and out of Homeland Security's interrogation rooms. He certainly doesn't think he'll be hassled again. Although Hasan Elahi has gone to extremes to prove his innocence online, there are plenty of instances in which the innocent have taken a hit to their reputation because of something posted online.

How the Innocent Can Take a Beating on Google: Some Examples

Nothing says "You can trust us with your money" like a reference to a major lawsuit you're involved in with a high-profile client on the first page of Google's search results when people type in the name of your money management firm.

I had firsthand experience with this when a former client of mine — a wealth management firm — called me one morning and said, "Harrison, do you think you could help us with a reputation issue we're having because of one of our clients?"

Their concern was a business wire posting that reported a lawsuit the firm had filed against a well-known recording artist in 2005 for extortion and civil conspiracy. The ugly post showed up on page 1 of Google's search results—and apparently had been there for years—whenever someone looked up information about the company on Google.

Even though my client was the one doing the suing, they concluded correctly that it looks terrible when the first impression someone gets upon researching a company is evidence of a contentious legal case in which that company is involved. Management kept putting the uncomfortable issue on the back burner, and the reputation-dinging search result was displayed prominently —four years after the report surfaced— on the first page of the most powerful search engine in the world. If you or your company is facing a similar threat to your reputation, don't delay in hopes that it will take care of itself. It won't. Instead, flood the search engines with up-to-date blogs, news, and articles about your company, its products and services, and its executives or leadership that push the damaging entry to the hinterland of pages—at least five or six pages down— where most searchers won't go.

Another client of mine, an accomplished entrepreneur who planned on entering the political arena as a conservative, once asked me for my input on a political consultant he'd planned on hiring. The consultant seemed to have excellent credentials at first glance, but a three-minute Google search produced a dating advertisement he had posted on a message board that went into great detail about the qualities he was looking for in the person he wanted to date. My client rejected the consultant on the basis of what he considered extremely poor judgment for a professional in sharing this type of personal information so openly. After all, this consultant's job was first and foremost to manage the professional reputation of his clients; that's probably tough to do for a consultant who has trouble managing his own reputation.

Then there's the story of a female CFO candidate, as reported in a *US News & World Report* article, who was in the job market. The woman—a Harley rider—had posted photos of herself on a motorcycle, wearing little clothing and a whole bunch of tattoos. Kathy Simmons, the CEO of Netshare, a job-hunting Web site that was interviewed for the article, said she would question the woman's professional judgment if she considered hiring her and found those photos.

Unfortunately, it's very difficult, if not impossible, to keep one's personal life and professional image separate online. Yet with the proliferation of all the social networking sites we discussed in Chapter 10, such as Facebook, MySpace, and any number of dating Web sites, the need for keeping a check on self-disclosure has become a matter of astute reputation management.

Why Search Engines Can Make or Break Your Reputation and What You Can Do to Influence Public Perception

> *Google is not a search engine. It's a reputation management system. Online your rep is quantifiable, findable and totally unavoidable.* — Wired *magazine*

Google doesn't give specific numbers—for competitive reasons, it says—but estimates put the number of Google searches per day anywhere from 700 million to 2 billion. Chances are that someone is googling you right now.

That's especially true if you're in the job market. Whether you're a recent college graduate or a C-level executive, you have a bull's-eye on your application that says "Search me." That's the case because potential employers are concerned about skeletons in your closet and about the things you're not telling them, particularly since the average curriculum vitae is a hyped-up highly biased description of oneself, mixed with a few half-truths and the occasional outright fabrication. Therefore, they trek online—according to recent research, a staggering 35 percent of hiring managers use Google to do online background checks on job candidates—and dig up what they can before unofficially giving you a yea or nay for the next round. Others in the reputation management field report the total number of online searches on job candidates by potential employers at more than 77 percent.

Underscoring the point that reputation is in the forefront of the minds of professionals and executives everywhere, recent research by the New York–based global public relations firm Weber Shandwick reports that a resounding 100 percent of chief executives and chairpersons frequently think about the reputations of their companies. Among the findings are data that show that corporate CEOs and chairpersons are concerned primarily about critics, disgruntled employees, and dissatisfied customers waging disparaging online campaigns against their companies, whereas executives below the C-level are most worried about the leaking of confidential information onto the Internet. Negative media coverage about company performance in a perilous economy is another concern that keeps executives awake at night.

Considering the cyberthreats to your reputation and the pressing need to manage public perception, the following material provides three critical proactive steps every executive and professional can take online to avoid the wide-ranging effects of any amount of loss of one's corporate or personal reputation.

1. Mind Your Web Site

First of all, it's important to have one. If you are one of the few holdouts who think that your customers don't look for you online, get with it. When someone types your name into a search engine, you want that Web site to be the first line of defense in the reputation game. A Web site says who you are and what you do and — by design — how you think of yourself. At the very least your Web site will take one of the top spots — on the coveted first page — of Google's listing that provide a reference to your name. You get to decide the message your brand sends here. Add to this the fact that according to research by Weber Shandwick on online reputation, 99 percent of executives consider corporate Web sites their prime source of information about a company, whether they seek data on competitors, vendors, suppliers, or business partners.

The results of executives' subsequent evaluations that are based on a company's online presence add to the impressions they form about that company's reputation. Weber Shandwick's finding that top executives place high value on a well-designed Web site to keep reputations in the clear should induce every corporate stakeholder or executive decision maker to log on to his or her online domain to reevaluate the message it sends to people who are dropping in to find out who you are and what you're all about.

2. Start Blogging

You could do worse than emulate the online habits of John Chambers of Cisco, Bill Marriott of Marriott International, or Elon Musk, CEO of

Tesla Motors. They are among a growing set of blogging CEOs who don't just recognize the value of staying in the conversation with their constituents via social media methods but actually use the power of blogging to ward off potential online reputation assassins.

Tesla Motors' Elon Musk, addressing impending layoffs at his firm, preempted an anticipated onslaught by blog snipers by spilling the beans himself: "There will also be some headcount reduction due to consolidation of operations." Transparency and being proactive in disclosing bad news immediately can be a tremendous asset in influencing public perception online, as illustrated in a *New York Times* article titled "In Era of Blog Sniping, Companies Shoot First." The *Times* piece mentions Loïc Le Meur, founder of the video blogging site Seesmic, who had to let one-third of his staff go in October 2008. Rather than wait for others to break the news online and define the issue in their terms, which would have invited negative reaction by the blogging masses, Le Meur got in front of a camera and posted an emotional video, announcing the layoffs on his site before the grapevine had a chance to react. The comments he subsequently received were largely positive and supportive.

Whether you make announcements on a blog or on your corporate Web site, the point is that the impression you give should be one of openness and transparency as opposed to hiding and whitewashing. The great thing about blogs is that they rank very high, often on the first page of Google. Smart executives take advantage of one of the most powerful weapons in their battle for an unblemished reputation.

3. Launch a Good News Assault

The Internet is patient and welcoming of the good, the bad, and the ugly. Why not tip the odds in favor of the good? To protect your executive presence and manage perceptions, consider becoming an author. You don't have to occupy space on the *New York Times* bestseller list—although it doesn't hurt—to flood Google with honorable mentions on all kinds of Web sites. However, authoring the blogs, along with professional articles, white papers, all types of reviews, and news releases with an authoritative quote, can crowd out reputation busters that fight for space on page 1 of Google. Similarly, offering your expert commentary to mainstream media journalists and pundits will get you quoted online in more places than one. Although the immediate goal is to boost your reputation online, the strategies described above can help you stay on the good side of your constituents as any potential dings to your reputation stay tucked away on page 6 of the search engine.

The Seven Most Common Mistakes That Sabotage People's Reputations Online and How to Avoid Them

1. Careless Social Networking

Accept the reality that the Internet is open to everyone and that pictures, video clips, online profiles, and other personal information will be seen by people to whom you wouldn't show them in the offline world. Posting unguarded images and content on Web sites such as Facebook, MySpace, and YouTube tends to inflict harm on people's reputations when they least expect it. If you decide to create your own pages and profiles on any of the social networking sites, consider the fact that even the profiles of your friends and others you link to can have equally embarrassing consequences even if you monitor your own content closely. It's time to ax the friends with drunken party pictures and remove the video of the boating and sunbathing trip in Spain if you care about your reputation.

2. Compromising E-Mails

Research from the trenches conducted by Weber Shandwick and the Economist Intelligence Unit has revealed that 87 percent of global executives have sent or received an electronic message (private e-mail, text, or Twitter) by mistake. The research further states that although some e-mails are sent by accident, about one in four executives report that they've forwarded a private e-mail to someone else on purpose. Considering the millions of e-mails that are sent daily, the potential for reputation-dinging e-mail fallout is disconcerting to say the least.

The solution, besides making doubly sure you don't accidentally hit the "reply-all" button, send e-mails in a heightened emotional state, or share confidential information with unauthorized others, may be more technology. You can install outbound e-mail monitoring technology—if you're working for a larger organization, chances are that it is already in place—or rely on your colleagues to monitor your e-mails for you. The e-mail security provider Proofpoint commissioned a study carried out by Forrester Research that found that 41 percent of organizations with 20,000 or more employees have staff on payroll that either read your e-mails, with their attention trained on confidential information you may be leaking intentionally or by accident or analyze your e-mails automatically via e-mail auditing technology.

When you're the boss, even that technology may not help. John Mackey, the CEO of Whole Foods Market, had a major lapse in judgment when he wrote an e-mail to his board about the potential acquisition of the competitor Wild Oats Markets, labeling the move "the elimination of a rival." That kind of language violated federal regulations and promptly landed Mackey in hot water, primarily because the errant e-mail made its way onto the desks of the Federal Trade Commission. However, this was not Mackey's only blunder, as you'll see below. There are clearly a number of ways in which you can harm your reputation via e-mail, the least of which will have you being called out by corporate monitors for violating their e-mail policy. That could get you fired.

3. Controversial Blogging

It's bad when a line employee does it—companies frown upon this, frequently firing the offending blogger—but it's a bona fide reputation killer when a top-level executive does it. Back to e-mailer and Whole Foods chief John Mackey, who also turned out to be behind years of anonymous blog postings that, among other unflattering things, questioned the value of competitor Wild Oats' stock, even predicting impending bankruptcy for that company, all with the intention to buy Wild Oats once the shares hit rock bottom.

The NPR program *All Things Considered* reported on its Web site that the Whole Foods CEO's online conduct was considered "unethical and embarrassing" by business and legal experts. His controversial blogging practice earned Mackey a subsequent SEC investigation and a permanent stain on his reputation. Advocating what you believe in in your blog postings is a good way to build your reputation. Make sure that it is done ethically, with transparency, and that it doesn't conflict with your brand message or it will end up burning you in the search engines.

4. Leaked Memos

Leaks to the media often come in form of memorandums whose unintended disclosure can have embarrassing consequences for their authors. Of course, the likelihood that they'll end up online with the author's name in boldface is as certain as an eastern sunrise. There's the *New York Times* report of a memo that was intended for the French diplomatic corps by the British ambassador to Afghanistan, leaked to the French media, predicting that the NATO-led military campaign against the Taliban would fail. The ambassador added that the best solution for the country would be to install an "acceptable dictator," according to the French paper that received the leak. Google Sir Sherard Cowper-Coles and witness the British ambassador to Kabul's permanent gaffe on his online résumé.

Not an issue for the average C-level executive? Then consider a *Wall Street Journal* report about Yahoo!'s CEO, Carol Bartz. The newly installed chief executive was upset that someone at Yahoo! leaked her first companywide memo to the media, after which she sent an admonishing memo to the staff that promptly made its way to the media. In the second leaked memo she referenced the first one by writing, "Plug the leaks" and "I hope whoever did it, feels bad enough to come forward and resign." She added, "Maybe we should have a weekly bounty on such people. I will throw in the first thousand dollars." The full memo includes other frank language that the CEO clearly wouldn't want the public to see. It's obviously embarrassing for the new Yahoo! chief, and until she gets the issue under control, she has to anticipate that any internal communication may find its way to the outside. The perception that is created from the start, dinging her reputation, is that she has no control over her staff at Yahoo!. The solution is likely to involve a more intimate dialogue with staffers until they respect her enough to stop sabotaging her communication efforts.

5. Misstatements and Fabrications

One of the most reputation-damaging and embarrassing mistakes executives make that inevitably get plastered all over the Internet are outright lies or fabrications of facts. Bloomberg News reported a story in which Microsemi CEO James Peterson had lied in SEC documents about having earned two degrees from Brigham Young University. The university, however, confirmed that Peterson received no degrees from it. To make matters worse, the CEO initially went on the offensive, denying the accusations in an issued press release titled "Microsemi's CEO Peterson Denies Misrepresenting Degrees from BYU."

In the release, Peterson stated that he "categorically" denied having misrepresented his degrees. That came after Bloomberg News first reported the allegations. Since then, chip maker Microsemi's stock has dropped 54 percent. Peterson's punishment, according to Bloomberg, was to pay $100,000 to the company and forgo a bonus for the current fiscal year. In addition, Microsemi reportedly will delay vesting the CEO's stock grants by one year. There is no question that the reputation loss Peterson suffered will be the biggest cost of his fabrications.

Charles Elson, director of the University of Delaware's John L. Weinberg Center for Corporate Governance, has weighed in on the issue in a message that has been posted online, of course: "It's not the degree, or lack thereof, it's the misstatement to the board and the public that's the issue." He added, "When this has happened at other companies, the CEO has been terminated." Whether or not this CEO ultimately will regain the trust of his board and his shareholders, the damage to his and the company's reputation is done and visible for anyone who's able to type his name into a search engine. Hundreds of postings are waiting to tell the story.

6. Slow or No Reaction to Rumors and Criticism

Here again we can learn from the corner office of the executive suite what not to do in an era in which everyone has a voice and everyone will be heard. Take former Home Depot CEO Robert Nardelli, who was criticized in the media for his enormous compensation package—$200 million plus—when the company hadn't been performing well for years.

Nardelli, however, who was prone to stonewalling the media and even openly encouraged his directors to boycott a pivotal annual shareholders meeting in 2006 because of an anticipated PR attack by organized labor, did nothing to silence his critics. His lack of communication and perceived arrogant behavior became the focus of most of the media coverage Home Depot received, describing its CEO as a "poster-child for excessive executive compensation." News of Nardelli's $210 million severance package only reinforced that distinction when he was ousted from Home Depot just a few months after the 2006 shareholder debacle.

Then, in the top job at Chrysler, Nardelli seemed to repeat his mistakes by not being transparent about his pay at the auto giant. The headline in the *International Herald Tribune* said it all: "Chrysler CEO's Silence about His Pay Does Not Help Repair His Reputation." Stonewalling or hoping that bad press will die down and critics will move on to other things is wishful thinking, particularly when shareholders, interest groups, and the media, including bloggers, are keeping ever closer tabs on executive compensation and wheeling and dealing on Wall Street. A clear and transparent communication strategy is in order to protect one's own reputation and that of the organization one represents.

7. Lack of Executive Presence on the Web

I mentioned earlier the importance of having a well-designed Web site because of research findings that the vast majority of executives look for information and overall impressions about others on the Web. The quality of your presence on the Web is the first and often only chance you get to project credibility and earn initial respect. This need to impress is exacerbated by the fact that people have infinite choices for providers of just about any type of service or product presented online as well as the reality that people make a snap decision—within seconds—about whether they want to explore a relationship with you further.

A well-designed and structurally sound Web site is not necessarily cheap, though it doesn't have to be prohibitively expensive either. When approaching a design firm, make sure that your brand message shines through in every aspect of your site and that the user experience is first and foremost in the site builder's mind. You will have to provide this information to them in the context of your customers' stories and the experiences they are looking for from your company.

In Chapter 15 we will delve deeper into the art and science of reputation management and tell you what to do when you're faced with a crisis that threatens to destroy your reputation and limit your chances of achieving a stellar executive presence.

15

Reputation Management 2.0

What Constitutes a Reputation Crisis?

One of the biggest challenges—and opportunities—that can befall a business executive is a crisis that tests his or her leadership and decision-making skills, with the final score open to scrutiny. This is where one's executive presence is put on trial, asserted or destroyed. If you haven't learned how to deal with a crisis situation, your first experience probably will be an unpleasant surprise. Many people harbor misconceptions about a crisis: what it will look like and how to deal with it. These misconceptions impair their ability to respond appropriately and effectively. By the time they understand where they've gone wrong, it's too late. Fortunately, you can avoid that fate. By understanding the truth about some of the most common myths about crises, you will have the advantage when a crisis strikes.

Read on and find out whether you've fallen victim to some of those myths about crises.

The Top Five Misconceptions about a Crisis Situation

Myth 1: If you Ignore the Media, They Will Move on and Forget about It

Ignoring the media is the worst thing you can do. Reporters tend to be inquisitive, and when they don't get answers to their questions, they ask more questions. A small crisis, if properly handled with the media, frequently becomes a nonissue, but if it is handled improperly, it can turn into a big story as every reporter asks, "What are they trying to hide?"

An infamous example is Citigroup CEO Vikram Pandit's response to a question by a member of the House Committee on Financial Services on February 11, 2009. The House member asked the Citi CEO "how much salary he received in 2008" and "how much bonus or other financial considerations" he received in 2008. Pandit's response was, "My compensation for the year 2008 was my salary, which was $1 million," and "I received no bonuses." At the expense of Pandit's rapidly dwindling executive presence and personal credibility, Reuters reported his actual compensation for 2008 just a month later, on March 16. The Citigroup chief had been awarded a total of $10.82 million in compensation for 2008, which didn't look nearly as good as his stated 2008 compensation of $1 million—against a backdrop of Citi's acceptance of $45 billion in bailout funds over the previous five months—when it was asked about by the committee member Dennis Moore in February. The difference in compensation was made up for by sign-on and retention awards Pandit received shortly after taking the helm at Citigroup; this technically was not a bonus, but it certainly matched the description of "financial consideration" in the question.

Although the CEO may not have been lying in a strict legal sense, he clearly was guilty of subterfuge, and that is precisely how the public and the House committee and the probing member who asked the question perceived it. Perception, as you have learned throughout this book, is always someone's reality. In this case, Pandit's perceived fib is played over and over on video-sharing sites and rehashed in news articles and blogs for all to see and shake their collective heads over.

The moral of this story and many others like it is that if the media do not receive what they consider adequate closure on a question, scandal, or event, newsmakers will continue to mention the issue in every story they publish on you and your organization until the matter is cleared up. Perceived transparency is the key when one is dealing with the media.

Myth 2: Real Crises Are Sudden Disasters That Immediately Make Headlines

For organizations that have been lucky enough not to experience a crisis, their main experience with corporate crisis is what they see in the news. Obviously, their perception of crisis is skewed toward the kinds of issues that already are making headlines. For this reason, they may believe that they're safe, unaware of the dozens of crises that other corporations deal with behind the scenes. If the organization is lucky, the crisis will stay behind the scenes. Unfortunately, this means that it's easier to learn from others' mistakes than from their successes.

The takeaway here is not to think you're safe just because your organization isn't in the news. A backstage crisis may be festering just below the surface. It's in your interest to be aware of these crises too.

Myth 3: Admitting Guilt or Culpability Will Make Things Worse

When dealing with a crisis, some companies mistakenly adopt a purely legal strategy. Perhaps they think they'll fare better if they avoid admitting fault. This may be a good strategy to follow in a court of law, but it's usually the wrong strategy to follow in the court of public opinion.

Taking responsibility often saves a company from a PR disaster. Not only that, this strategy may head off legal problems before they begin. By establishing a strong, supportive relationship with stakeholders in the crisis, a company frequently can avoid the adversarial mindset that leads to lawsuits. In contrast, failure to accept responsibility or apologize has taken many companies down a long, nightmarish road of extended lawsuits and damaged reputations.

Myth 4: Most Crises Are Caused by an Employee Mistake or a Natural Disaster

These types of crises often are highly publicized. Their simplicity and controversy make for good headlines. However, the most common and crippling crises generally stem from internal conflicts or management problems. Top-rank management generally has an interest in not recognizing or acknowledging this type of crisis, and so the situation escalates. For this reason, these conflicts are frequently the most damaging to companies in the long term. When the crisis finally is made public, angry consumers are much more likely to take the company to task, holding senior-level management accountable.

Myth 5: Only Big Corporations Need a Plan for Crisis Communication

Small and even midsize corporations often persuade themselves not to worry about a plan for crisis. They tell themselves that it won't happen to them, and if it does, they'll deal with it then. This "cross that bridge when we come to it" syndrome can be dangerous for the long-term survival of an organization or company. A popular saying in crisis communication management circles goes: "When it's raining, it's too late to build the ark."

Crisis Intelligence 101: How to Recognize the Many Faces of a Potential Crisis

Now you know the five biggest myths about crises, but will you recognize a crisis when it strikes close to home? For organizations and companies, crises can come in many different forms. Many companies and executives fail to respond effectively to a crisis when it's not the one they were expecting or doesn't fit within their frame of reference as far as crisis situations are concerned. For this reason, it's important to keep an open mind and fine-tune your perceptual acuity and crisis radar. Realize that crises can sneak up on you in many shapes and forms. The sections below explore some of the many forms a crisis can take.

1. Accusations Spread by a Customer, Whether True or False

In today's world, many potential customers use review sites on the Internet to get information about a company or product. On the Internet, one disgruntled customer spreading misinformation or false accusations can have a tremendous reach. Depending on the size of your business, this could pose a serious problem.

2. A Damaging Story Run by an Investigative Reporter or Influential Bloggers

The scandal involving former North Carolina Senator John Edwards and his alleged affair with a staffer was brought to public attention through the efforts of the *National Enquirer* and conservative bloggers. Afterward, it was picked up quickly by mainstream media outlets.

3. New Government Regulations That Affect the Way You Do Business

In 1990, the California Air Resources Board adopted a new set of regulations for vehicle emissions. The regulations required that by 1998, at least 2 percent of all the vehicles sold in California be zero-emission vehicles. (The regulations eventually were relaxed because of lobbying by automakers.)

4. Confidential Information Being Leaked

A much publicized PR and legal crisis involved Hewlett-Packard spying on its board members through illegal and unethical means. The crisis started when HP realized that confidential information was being leaked by a board member. If it had had a better plan in place to deal with that possibility, it might not have resorted to questionable means and would have avoided the ensuing legal fracas that cost several people their jobs.

5. Serious Injury or Accident Harming an Employee

The 2005 BP Texas City disaster is a significant example of this. Fifteen employees were killed and over 170 were injured in an explosion and fire at a BP refinery. Don't forget that small companies can have worker injuries even if they just have a small warehouse in the back.

6. Serious Injury or Accident Caused by an Employee

Let's say you run a florist shop. Your employee, a delivery driver, could get in an accident in a company car, fatally injuring a pedestrian.

7. Criminal Trials and Legal Proceedings

An example of this would be the highly publicized corporate fraud scandal and legal trials that pushed the successful company Enron into bankruptcy and put the accounting giant Arthur Andersen out of business.

8. Civil Lawsuits and Legal Proceedings

After the BP Texas City disaster mentioned above, a woman who lost both parents in the accident sued BP, in part to bring more public exposure to the circumstances of the accident. The case was not settled until over a year and a half later.

9. Organized Demonstrations or Protests against Organizations

Example: The New York Police Department faced a wave of bad PR after an unarmed man was gunned down by police officers on his wedding day. In an organized protest, over 200 demonstrators gathered outside a precinct in Queens, New York.

10. Chemical or Environmental Accidents

An example is the Exxon Valdez oil spill in 1989. Between 10 million and 30 million gallons of oil were spilled into the Prince William Sound along the Alaska coastline.

11. Death or Illness of a Key Executive

In 2004, Steve Jobs, the CEO of Apple Computer, underwent surgery to remove a cancerous tumor from his pancreas. The company faced the important task of communicating effectively with employees about the issue as well as assuring stockholders of Jobs's health and continued contributions to the company. Jobs then took another medical leave of absence that made Apple shareholders nervous about his health. Jobs's less than transparent communication about his illness did nothing to calm their fears.

12. Unfounded, Untraceable Rumors.

In 2004, an anonymous e-mail circulated on the Internet, claiming that the sender's dog had died from liver failure caused by being exposed to Swiffer WetJet products. The e-mail also alleged that Swiffer WetJet was harmful to pets. The allegations were proved false by both Procter & Gamble and the ASPCA's Animal Poison Control Center, but by that time many pet owners had seen the e-mail.

13. Natural Disasters.

Untold numbers of businesses in the area were destroyed by Hurricane Katrina as their assets literally washed away and their customer bases vanished as they were displaced or impoverished or forced to move to other parts of the country.

14. Allegations of Racial or Sexual Discrimination.

If not handled properly, these allegations can turn quickly into lawsuits. For example, in 1994 accusations of pervasive racist policies and hiring practices at Texaco turned into a class-action lawsuit brought by 1,400 minority employees and eventually settled for $176 million. Walmart faced a sexual discrimination lawsuit brought by 1.6 million employees, the largest discrimination case in history.

15. Strikes or Disruption of Labor Practices.

On December 20, 2005, New York City Transit Authority workers went on strike, shutting down the transit system for a couple of days. The crisis for the city was compounded by the fact that local retailers were depending on dollars spent by last-minute Christmas shoppers, many of whom had trouble finishing their shopping without access to public transportation.

It should be clear now that crises can take many shapes and forms. It's practically impossible to anticipate every negative event that may occur, but you should try to anticipate as many different potential crisis situations as you can. You never know where conflict will arise. You can avoid being caught by surprise by giving careful thought to the possibilities: how certain circumstances may affect your business and how those circumstances should be handled.

Frequently, an incorrectly handled crisis will morph into another kind of crisis altogether. Consider, for example, the BP Texas City Disaster in 2005 that was mentioned above. It may seem to be one protracted incident, but in fact the crisis took place on three levels.

The company failed to follow health and safety regulations. Although this was brought to the attention of management several times in the months before the accident, they failed to act appropriately. At this point, its was a backstage crisis, fed by both health and safety issues and management neglect.

Then the actual accident occurred, killing and injuring employees. At this point, the crisis became live, making headlines.

The company failed to communicate adequately with stakeholders in the crisis and took an adversarial position against the victims. That led to a third crisis: the hard-fought lawsuit that made headlines for months.

The company had multiple opportunities to make different, better choices in terms of how it handled the crisis. If it had identified the crisis at step 1 and fixed the backstage problems, the crisis never would have made headlines and lives would have been saved. What's the important lesson here?

When planning your response to any crisis situation, keep in mind the repercussions. Ask yourself: Will this response create another crisis?

Earlier in this chapter we mentioned backstage crises and live crises. Though they are different, each is equally deserving of your careful attention and a considered communications plan.

Live crises are the ones that occur without warning, generating immediate news coverage. Often the company and the media will learn about the problem simultaneously. A high-profile accident, an environmental incident, whistleblowing, and a labor strike fall into this category. These types of crises happen to politicians and celebrities too. A public outburst or a statement taken out of context can become a major story practically as soon as the words leave the speaker's mouth. See Chapter 12 for examples of unfortunate sound bites.

Backstage crises, in contrast, fester beneath the surface. For weeks, months, or even years, perhaps only a few members of the company are aware of the issue. However, these issues have the potential to become major crises if they are discovered, and so they should be treated as accordingly. Examples include internal allegations of discrimination, operational problems, and fraudulent accounting practices. When brought to light by the media, these problems have the potential to become major corporate scandals with dire consequences for everyone associated with the organization. This is the time when executive presence can be asserted or diminished, depending on one's mental agility and level of preparation.

When handled effectively, backstage crises can be prevented from seeing the light of day. If you identify the problem early, come up with a plan to correct it, and do correct it, your problem will never make the headlines.

In contrast, you will have little time to devise a plan to deal with a live crisis, and so it's important to have a plan outlined ahead of time. With your approach already sketched out and on file, you can summon a quick and resolute response to whatever happens. If you respond in a timely manner, you have a much better chance of weathering the storm and salvaging your reputation, perhaps even giving it a boost for making the right decisions under pressure.

The next section offers practical strategies for dealing with both backstage and live crises.

Dealing with Crisis: How to Prevent the Smoke from Becoming a Fire

In dealing with any crisis, your response should always be two-pronged, with an operational response and a communication response. The way you face the issue can have a major impact on the way you're perceived by your key constituencies, from direct reports and colleagues to bosses and shareholders. To protect your executive presence and gain everyone's respect, your plan should include two parts:

1. What are you going to do to correct the problem?
2. How are you going to communicate the problem and the solution to your stakeholders and the public?

These two aspects of the plan should be devised, considered, and implemented together in one smooth and powerful response.

Some companies make the mistake of focusing too narrowly on the operational response. They take steps to resolve the issue, but because they do not communicate effectively with the public about their actions, the response fails. The public perceives the company to be unavailable and unaccountable, causing a potentially bigger secondary crisis.

Some companies, in contrast, make the mistake of focusing too much on the communications response. They offer statements to the public, sounding sincere and concerned, but if their actions fail to support their statements, their initial message will ring false. In this situation too a backlash against the company can cause a secondary crisis that could have been contained with the appropriate action.

The following section offers directions and strategies for your crisis communications plan. These steps are necessary elements in dealing with the initial crisis. Think of them as a road map with a series of directions to be followed in the correct order. The playbook steps listed afterward take individual circumstances into account, offering potential approaches for a variety of situations.

Reputation in Peril: A Road Map for Effective Crisis Management

1. Anticipate the Crisis and Have a Plan in Place Beforehand

Like the Boy Scouts, communications experts have a rule: Be prepared. It's impossible to overestimate the importance of planning for as many different kinds of situations as possible. You never know what scenario the future might throw at you.

My colleague Susan Tellem shared some of the strategies her firm uses to help prepare its clients for possible crises. Not only do they write manuals to follow in case of a crisis, they help their clients rehearse crisis scenarios as if they were really happening. One year their firm conducted a two-day crisis prep training session with a pharmaceutical company in which they kidnapped the CEO! Senior management (and the CEO himself, presumably) knew that it was a test run, but the majority of the company's employees did not. My colleague said, "It was not a joke, it was serious, and we wanted to make everyone react as if they would had it been real, so that they were really prepared." She recounted how thoroughly everyone got into the moment. They wrote mock press releases, spoke with pretend media, and simulated the crisis as accurately as they could. Even those who were part of the training had to pinch themselves as a reminder that the kidnapping wasn't real.

This story provides two important messages. First, you have to be creative when you are anticipating a crisis. Second, your plan should include as much detail as possible. No matter what size your company is—small, medium, or large—you should have a detailed, well-considered manual with your crisis plan. "Most of the people I deal with have no idea that something like this is going to hit," this colleague noted. Today's organizations have to be prepared for anything.

2. When a Crisis Hits, Ask Questions; Don't Act until You Have All the Facts

It's impossible to count the executives who have gotten themselves in trouble by giving a statement to the media before they were informed fully about the situation. Beyond that, it's impossible to formulate a plan of attack before you know exactly what you're dealing with. As soon as you get your first inkling of disaster, investigate the situation in as much detail as time allows. Only then can you begin to deal with the problem with confidence and accuracy.

Gil Bashe, another colleague, underscored this message. In approaching a crisis situation, Bashe said, "the first rule is, really analyze the facts. Get details. Any good communication plan, response, activity, starts with the truth and a complete understanding of all the relevant information."

3. Picture the Ideal Outcome

You have all the facts, and now you're ready to start making a plan. Not so fast. Before you reach the planning stages, it's useful to spend some time considering where you want to end up when the crisis is over. How do you envision your organization once the issue is behind you?

Bashe agreed about this point as well: "It's essential to look at the outcomes, the identity the company wants to create through its communications. . . . We have to act appropriately here, for the outcome."

What impression do you want to leave with your consumers and the public? What relationship do you want to have with your stakeholders? Where do you want to end up in the marketplace? Once you can articulate these goals, you may find that your plan practically writes itself. Impulsively responding to crisis can lead to a knee-jerk reaction. Striving to accomplish a particular set of goals can make the solution to your baffling problem seem self-evident. There's an old expression, "When you don't know where you want to go, any road will get you there." The reverse is true too: If you know where you want to go, you know what road will take you from where you are to where you want to be.

4. Be Available

In a crisis situation, many leaders and executives make the mistake of battening the hatches and hunkering down, out of sight. However, the worst thing you can do is say "no comment" when reporters come knocking.

Instead, you should go out of your way to be available to both the media and any stakeholders involved in the situation. Refusing to speak to the media or communicate openly with customers or stakeholders can escalate the initial crisis into a secondary crisis, as was illustrated in our earlier examples. Conversely, being open and honest with the public often can defuse a crisis. Human curiosity is a powerful thing. Sometimes just answering questions candidly can turn a scandal into a nonstory.

This is what happened to a client of Susan Tellem's. The client had been involved in Medicare fraud, and the case went to trial. Although this clearly was a difficult situation, Susan tried to maintain open communications with the media. She made a list of 20 reporters who covered that kind of story and made a practice of consistently reaching out to them, providing any available updates. Then, when the verdict was handed down, she immediately called all the reporters and told them what the penalty had been. The sentence turned out to be relatively mild in comparison to what they'd feared. More important, Susan's honesty with the media defused interest in the issue. She said, "Lo and behold, only one magazine reported on it. . . . By being out there and calling them right away, I think we defused a lot of the bomb. Only one publication ran the story, and it ran it in a rather balanced way. So I was very proud of the way it was handled."

5. Every Team Member Should Work on Implementing the Plan

Successful crisis communication is always a team effort. Make sure every team member is on the same page, assign parts of the plan to as many competent people as you can get on board, and move ahead.

These five steps constitute the road map. Make them part of your immediate response to any crisis. Flexible yet crucial, they lay the bedrock for a successful response.

The next five strategies are more specialized. They are suggestions for various ways to deal with a crisis. Unlike the previous directions, which are intended to be used together to create a total approach, the playbook offers mix-and-match strategies. Their usefulness is highly dependent on the details of the situation. How you use them and when will depend on the specific scenario, your understanding of your market or constituents, and your organizational culture. The goal is to give you an understanding of the different types of strategies available for defusing a crisis.

The Playbook: Top Strategies for Protecting Your Good Name

1. Admit the Problem, Take Responsibility for It, and Correct It

If the organization is at fault for the crisis, this is almost certainly the right course of action. Of course, not all crises imply wrongdoing on the part of the organization. Difficult new legal regulations and false rumors spread by a competitor are two examples of exceptions. If the situation is one in which the organization has made a mistake, the best thing to do is to come clean. You should own up to your responsibility and express your sincere empathy and concern to whoever has been hurt by the mistake. Then do your best to correct the issue and ensure that it never happens again.

An important detail to note here is that the organization needs to take responsibility as a whole. Making employees into scapegoats or trying to lay blame frequently will backfire. Instead, the company should come together as a team, taking responsibility for what happened and vowing to correct it. If one or two persons were to blame, appropriate action should be taken against those individuals, but the company simultaneously should apologize for the environment and the infrastructure that allowed the situation to happen.

My colleague Sarah Spaulding discussed this point in relation to a situation faced by a former client of hers. The client, a medical institution, experienced a tragic event: a helicopter crash: "The helicopter hit power lines and then crashed. It would have been really easy to blame the pilot. . . . But instead we talked about the tragedy, we talked about the pilot's good flying record, the safe history of this helicopter service, and how this was just a tragic accident. Then we talked about the crisis procedures that could be put in place so this wouldn't happen in the future."

In a situation like this, your first job is to communicate concern for the victims of the accident, their family members, and anyone affected by the tragedy. Your second job is to communicate your organization's commitment to ensuring that the situation won't happen again.

Suzanne Bates also expressed the importance of taking responsibility and expressing concern. "This is where the lawyers and communications people get into heated conversations sometimes," she admitted. "The lawyers are never going to want you to take responsibility for anything, yet many times if you take responsibility for the piece you own, it defuses the crisis and in many ways mitigates your risks, even of legal action."

2. Surprise the Media

Sometimes the best way to deflect the media's attention is by surprising them with the unexpected. Challenging reporters' preconceptions can turn a negative story into a positive one or at least buy you some extra time.

The public relations expert Ned Barnett shared a story with me about how he managed to help a client do just that. The client, a college, had just been formed by a merger between two different schools. The two schools had used different pay systems for their employees. One was on a 9-month pay system, with slightly larger payments dispersed each month; the other was on a 10-month pay system, with slightly smaller payments. When they merged, the new payment system basically offered the worst of both worlds to the employees, who now got paid the smaller payments on a 9-month schedule. The employees decided to sue the college.

However, after investigating the issue, Barnett discovered that the new pay schedule had been mandated by the state. There wasn't much the school could do about it. Rather than being combative about the lawsuit, they decided to call a press conference to announce that they were filing an amicus curiae ("friend of the court") brief on behalf of their employees, supporting their claims. This turn of events caught the media off guard and helped generate goodwill toward the school.

3. Change the Subject

Politicians and celebrities are the acknowledged masters of this strategy. It should be used only with extreme care. If the crisis is more smoke than fire or is the type of scandal that will fizzle out quickly, changing the subject can be an effective way of deflecting media attention until the storm blows over. It is a way to get your organization out of the headlines for a few days; this may be important if your business or cause relies heavily on public opinion.

When former North Carolina Senator John Edwards made headlines for an alleged affair with a female staffer, most of the attention concerned his lying to the media about the affair in press conferences when pressed on the issue. However, Edwards changed the subject by announcing that he did not want to be a distraction during Barack Obama's presidential campaign.

"Not wanting to be a distraction" or "going into rehab" can be an effective way to change the subject when one is caught engaging in bad behavior. Of course, this trend has created a downside by offering fodder for late-night comedians.

However, there are few better strategies to avoid a scalding negative publicity bath that hurts the company's earnings than to change the subject, at least for a while. The following big business example demonstrates this.

Siemens AG, the German engineering juggernaut, never put too much effort—or funding—into advertising. That was the case until a corruption scandal rocked the firm—corporate executives were alleged to be paying bribes for infrastructure contracts around the world—and inspired its senior management to change the subject of public and media discourse and launch a major global public relations campaign to the tune of $450 million over three years. The campaign was designed to focus the public's attention on what Siemens does best, touting its technology advances in the areas of energy, industry, and health care. The aggressive $150-million-a-year effort that teamed the German conglomerate with the public relations powerhouse Ogilvy & Mather reportedly included advertising in print, on billboards, and on television, along with online marketing, in a concerted effort to change the subject and restore the company's formerly excellent reputation.

Changing the subject is a complicated, somewhat iffy, and, as in the example above, sometimes exorbitantly expensive strategy. Politicians use it with varying degrees of success. If the goal is simply to deflect attention for a few days (a week is a long time in politics), it can work. For companies and business executives, it's a touchier strategy. Companies and their leaders have much longer reputations to protect. If they fail to resolve problems or deflect criticism satisfactorily, eventually consumers will go somewhere else. In other words, changing the subject may not be the best strategy for an organization with long-term considerations unless it has the coffers of a Siemens. Then it might work. The same thing goes for individual business leaders whose executive presence has been damaged by scandal, rumor, or other mischief. Throwing lots of money at a reputation problem can work if time and money are abundant. Make sure the good news about you outweighs the bad, and the dark clouds of perception may give way to bluer skies eventually.

4. Use Passion to Make Your Case

In the world of business and the world of politics, heartfelt convictions and passionate beliefs often feel like the exception rather than the rule. That may be why passion can be such an effective way to help the public understand your side of the story.

Perhaps this method is best illustrated by a Ned Barnett story. His client, a public hospital in Michigan, was in a tight situation with limited funds. One of its most critical services was a prenatal intensive care unit that took care of very fragile newborns and preemies. Then the underpaid nurses in the unit decided to go on strike, hoping for higher pay. Generally, in a situation such as this, the media side with the workers and the union that represents them. As Barnett said, "The typical thing to do in this situation is to hunker down and not get confrontational."

However, Barnett felt that the stakes were too high to do that. He decided to follow a wholly different strategy. "You're on your own," Barnett remembered his boss saying to him as he went out to speak to the press, because what Barnett was about to do was completely out of line with the conventional wisdom. Instead of appeasing the media, he brought some intensely emotional subject matter to present: pictures of the intensive care unit and the fragile infants in its care. He explained that the patients in this ward required very specialized and intensive care. These were not the kinds of patients who could go for a few days without the special help they needed, and nurses or staff from elsewhere in the hospital were not trained to care for the infants properly. Barnett didn't need to come out with it explicitly, but the subtext to his message was clear: If the nurses carried out the strike, they would kill babies. Also, he explained, the hospital did not have the funds to raise the nurses' salaries.

Barnett's ambitious, passionate approach to dealing with the media and the public worked. The media sided with the hospital, the national union disavowed the strike, and the local unions turned against it as well. The crisis was defused.

This approach won't work for everyone or in all circumstances, but if you're in a situation in which the stakes are high and you can claim the moral high ground, don't be afraid to share your emotional investment with the public. Passion is a powerful thing. If you can make your case with sincere emotion, you may find that the public is sympathetic to your cause.

5. Look for the Silver Lining

Great companies can emerge from the trial by fire of a crisis stronger than they were before. Although that may seem like small consolation in a stressful time, it's worth remembering. In fact, this step echoes one of the musts: picturing the ideal outcome. It's possible for a company to handle a negative situation with such grace that its response earns the public's respect.

The manufacturer of Tylenol is a perfect example of this type of company. In the middle of a Tylenol tampering scare in 1980s, the company went above and beyond its responsibilities to its customers, recalling millions of dollars worth of the product. Despite the scare, those actions earned them trust. Although their millions of dollars in losses were undoubtedly painful for their accountants that year, they quickly won back their market share. They continue to be one of the most trusted analgesic brands today, possibly in part because of their responsible actions during the crisis.

By keeping your ideal outcome in mind and searching for the silver lining, you may discover a way to shine even in the middle of a crisis. If there's any opportunity you can seize to connect with the public at this time, take it.

The next section will show how this plays out in real life.

Crucial Lessons from Movers and Shakers in the World Business

The Grounding of JetBlue

David Neeleman, former CEO and cofounder of JetBlue Airlines, learned from experience what it was like to hear from thousands of disappointed customers about what they thought of his airline during a wintery week from hell in February of 2007.

Up to that point, JetBlue enjoyed a stellar reputation as a low-cost carrier with high satisfaction ratings from customers, but that changed quickly on a not-so-average travel Wednesday when an anticipated ice storm hit the eastern part of the United States. Other carriers had planned ahead by letting travelers know that scheduled flights were canceled before the bad weather, but Neeleman's JetBlue bet on a break in the clouds and planned on conducting business as usual.

That decision proved catastrophic for the airline and the thousands of passengers who ended up stranded, tired, frustrated, and hostile toward JetBlue's understaffed front lines, which at times had to have security step in to contain irate customers. It wasn't over quickly, as the canceled flights added up to a thousand in just five days, according to a *New York Times* report.

The evening news channels were buzzing with accounts from angry passengers, many of whom were forced to stay on the planes—a total of nine packed planes as reported by the *Times*—which sat on the tarmacs at New York's JFK International Airport for more than six hours.

If you've ever been delayed or stranded because of an error by an airline, you can multiply that by five days and a thousand canceled flights and get an idea of the perception the frustrated travelers had of JetBlue.

The company's response after the fiasco, however, by many accounts elevated David Neeleman to the status of a business leader who gets it and whose example will be discussed in business schools for years to come.

The CEO of JetBlue, realizing that his and the airline's reputation were close to the brink, crafted and delivered an authentic apology that not only resonated with the thousands of travelers, friends, and family members affected by the weeklong operational breakdown but also included a number of commitments that assured customers that the airline would go out of its way to make sure it never would happen again.

Let's take a closer look at the substance and the style of the apology that Neeleman issued after the debacle at JFK that his airline, its employees, and thousand of travelers suffered through.

I've summarized Neelemans's apology letter below and added my comments and analysis in italicized sections.

Dear JetBlue Customers,

We are sorry and embarrassed. But most of all, we are deeply sorry.

Although saying "sorry" has rolled off tongues too easily for many CEOs after they have disappointed their constituents, Neeleman's use of the term is strengthened by placing extra emphasis—he repeats "deeply sorry"—in his opening statement. It comes across as believable.

Neeleman then acknowledged that it had been the carrier's "worst operational week" in its seven-year history. He acknowledged that passengers were stranded and delayed and had flights canceled because of a severe winter ice storm that "disrupted the movement of aircraft" and basically shut out pilots and crew members who needed to get to work to serve JetBlue's passengers.

Here he spells out the fact that he understands the ordeal passengers went through, and although he doesn't blame the storm for the passengers' plight—he takes responsibility for "the worst operational week in JetBlue's seven-year history"— he characterizes it as a "severe winter ice storm" to put the situation squarely in perspective for those affected, framing the situation in terms of extraordinary circumstances as opposed to operational failure under normal conditions, which would make the airline look even worse.

He went on to acknowledge that because of a busy Presidents Day weekend "rebooking opportunities were scarce" and that the hold times at their customer service number were "unusually long or not even available."

Here the CEO frames the operational failures in terms of a "busy Presidents Day weekend" and JetBlue's attempted "recovery efforts." He mentions "scarce rebooking opportunities" and "unusually long or unavailable hold times" for the company's 800 number to reaffirm his understanding of the details of the operational breakdown.

He stated again how sorry he was and said that he understood the "frustration and inconvenience" that customers experienced. He went on to state that the reason he founded JetBlue was to make air travel more enjoyable and less of a hassle. He acknowledged that the company did not deliver on that promise during the interruptions.

The first sentence is aimed directly at those who suffered through the ordeal. It's a personal apology that doesn't mince words. He then restates what the airline is supposed to represent—an important reminder to anchor in people's minds—and his acknowledgment that JetBlue let people down.

Neeleman went on to restate his commitment to JetBlue's customers in his letter, saying that a comprehensive plan was put in place to avoid service breakdown situations in the future and announcing the JetBlue Airways Customer Bill of Rights—the carrier's official commitment to its passengers—including the way interruptions will be handled and restitution paid from then on.

Besides the straightforward acknowledgment that you have screwed up, people want to know what you are going to do to make sure it will not happen again. An apology without a clear plan that addresses what will be different from now on rings hollow and insincere, as customers have heard it all before. Here actions truly speak louder than words. Obviously, the apologist has to follow through on those actions immediately.

In addition to the apology Neeleman posted on JetBlue's Web site, he posted a video on YouTube that assured customers that an examination of their operation had taken place and that important changes such as a passenger bill of rights were forthcoming. The three-minute video presentation was delivered by the CEO—not read from a teleprompter—with humility and sincerity. Response to the video, which was viewed close to 400,000 times, was overwhelmingly positive and supportive as a result of the CEO's personal effort to reach out to customers.

Here are a few more examples of companies and people who've suffered a blow to their reputation and the actions they've taken to position themselves for future success.

Dell Hell

The year 2005 was not Dell's year to win a customer service award, and one very unhappy customer made sure the world knew it by blogging about his experiences with the personal computer maker.

Already a frequently discussed topic in PC circles, Dell's slippage in customer satisfaction, which was confirmed by a University of Michigan study that year, caused an avalanche of like-minded sentiment when the tech blogger Jeff Jarvis ranted about the bad customer service he had received from Dell on his blog BuzzMachine.

Jarvis started blogging about his bad experience with Dell when a computer he purchased malfunctioned and Dell gave him the runaround instead of helping fix his problem—or his computer.

Soon after Jarvis's posts about Dell hit the blogosphere, thousands of others joined with complaints and negative comments about the company, causing a virtual and very real PR nightmare for the computer maker. Jarvis added an open letter to Michael Dell, summarizing his experience and expressing his disappointment in the company's customer service culture. Unfortunately for Dell, anyone looking for information on Dell computers online was led right to this bonanza of bad press.

Soon after Jarvis started his influential blog about his experience with Dell, the computer maker began to pay attention to its reputation online, embracing social media and communicating directly with customers in forums such as Dell Shares, direct2dell, and Your Blog, the official Dell blog.

Although Dell CEO Michael Dell hasn't taken up blogging personally to communicate with his constituents, word from the reputation research community is that Dell's reputation has recovered as a result of its online communication efforts, increased customer service staffing, and diligent response to any customer problems before they turn into a full-blown crisis as they did in 2005.

Disgraced RadioShack CEO Starts Fresh

Much media attention has been paid over the years to the fallout from senior executives lying about their education and the financial loss and damage to both the executives' and the company's reputations it caused.

One of those fibbing CEOs was former RadioShack chief executive Dave Edmondson, who claimed academic degrees on his résumé that he didn't have. Specifically, the newly appointed CEO claimed degrees in theology and psychology from a college in California.

A small Texas paper, the *Fort Worth Star-Telegram*, checked into the CEO's education claims on his résumé and exposed the fib. Although Edmondson did spent some time at the college—two semesters, according to the school's registrar—he never received a degree.

Barely two months after taking the top job at RadioShack, Edmondson resigned in the face of pressure from the board and the prospect of legal action as lawyers started investigating his claims at the request of the company.

After a period of reflection in the south of France, Edmondson didn't waste time and began his reinvention process by starting his own business in an entirely different category.

The venture, EasySale Inc., is a consignment service that sells items of at least $50 value on eBay for people who don't want to go through the trouble themselves. In the process the company makes house or business calls and picks up the items—large and small—in big trucks before appraising and photographing the items and posting them online.

According to a *Dallas News* article, Edmondson put $600,000 of his own money into the venture and hired close to a hundred people, including some former RadioShack colleagues.

From the looks of it, the former RadioShack CEO's second life and business are buzzing, with trucks on the road and items for sale on eBay. The company's Web site boasts of having found and consigned all kinds of unique items—including rare Lee Harvey Oswald–related documents—that no doubt have put cash into the sellers' and Edmondson's pockets.

Edmondson's comment to the *Dallas Morning News* could be a mantra for all those who are looking to reposition themselves after a reputation disaster: "I could have said, 'I quit,' or I could learn from my mistakes, use them, and not withdraw from the world."

Success can help build a new reputation and slowly cause the old reputation to fade into the background and lose its potency in defining who you are.

GE Cleans Up a Dirty Little Secret

General Electric has been one of the most admired and recognized companies, giving the world one of its celebrated super-CEOs, Jack Welch.

A major stain on GE's reputation has been its longtime dismal environmental record. Over three decades, from around 1947 to 1977, GE reportedly discharged as much as 1.3 million pounds of polychlorinated biphenyls (PCBs) into the Hudson River. After government pressure mounted and lawsuits were filed to get GE to help clean up the chemical pollution in the Hudson, GE under Jack Welch's leadership spent millions of dollars in legal fees to avoid taking any part in the cleanup. Instead, GE went on the offensive in the media, spending more millions to show that the likely results of a cleanup effort would be a stirring up of the chemical waste that was lodged in the river bottom. But that was then.

In 1999, 16 years after the New York state attorney general filed the government's first lawsuit against the company in connection with the dumped PCBs, GE paid a $250 million settlement in reference to claims about its chemicals being dumped into and polluting the Hudson.

In the last few years, the Environmental Protection Agency and GE under Jeff Immelt's leadership have negotiated a massive—and expensive—cleanup effort involving dredging that proposed that a significant stretch of the river be cleaned up by GE at its expense. Although there have been a number of well-reported delays, progress has been made, as documented on GE's Web site, and the company's new corporate social responsibility efforts have been aligned perfectly with new green business categories GE has entered, such as solar and wind energy.

With a program called Ecomagination, GE's leadership has moved to reposition itself and reinvent the juggernaut as a green company dedicated to, as Immelt puts it, "develop[ing] tomorrow's solutions such as solar energy, hybrid locomotives, fuel cells, lower-emission aircraft engines, lighter and stronger durable materials, efficient lighting, and water purification technology."

To show that it's not easy to erase memories of past mischief, consider the *New York Times*'s acidic response to GE's stated commitment to a cleaner and greener future in an article titled "Talking Green, Acting Dirty": "[W]hile General Electric's increased emphasis on clean technology will probably result in improved products and benefit its bottom line, Mr. Immelt's credibility as a spokesman on national environmental policy is fatally flawed because of his company's intransigence in cleaning up its own toxic legacy."

Consistency and actions that continue to support GE's green mission as well as its commitment to the Hudson River cleanup effort eventually will bring the naysayers around and lift GE's and Immelt's reputations above the noise.

In this chapter, you've learned about some strategies for crisis and reputation management. Through the examples of prominent players in business and politics, you've learned what to do and what not to do.

Remember that the number one rule for crisis communicators and executives who are concerned about their reputation is to anticipate and prepare. Your executive presence will be strengthened if you embrace the crisis communication plan discussed in this chapter to maintain your good standing when a crisis strikes. Remember also that you can repair your reputation and restore the luster to your developing executive presence and credibility once it has taken a hit. Just be patient and follow the steps best suited to your situation and you'll recover in time.

Conclusion

The Art of Commanding Respect Like a CEO

MANY PEOPLE, a lot of them card-carrying cynics, will tell you there are only two ways to reach the level of CEO, and in both cases you are born to it: You either share the last name of the founder and somehow managed not to get kicked out of grad school before the reigning relative stepped aside, or there is something about your presence that sets you apart, that makes you some combination of brilliant, charismatic, empathetic, smooth, persuasive, strategic, and full-on cool. Simon Cowell of *American Idol* fame, who possesses only a few of those attributes, refers to the latter criterion as the "it factor," and by implication one can conclude that you have it or you don't. Although that may be true in entertainment and athletics, the business and corporate world remains a place where, genetics aside, you can acquire and evolve the attributes of a CEO-level executive presence the old-fashioned way—you can learn them. If you practice them and put them to work in your career, they can take you to high places, including the boardroom.

As you've learned in reading this book, the factors that result in a career path leading to the top of the organization chart are unthinkably complex. They have as much to do with relationships and perceptions as they do with quantifiable data and performance analysis, with the latter being a discipline fraught with imprecise human perceptions. Although there are plenty of active leaders who are anything but charismatic and socially intelligent, the nature of leadership is changing (one has to look no farther than the White House to see this in play), and the style and effectiveness with which a leader interfaces with others can be a magnetic variable in his or her success. Charismatic leaders understand the principles of perception: how people take in and filter sensory input and assign meaning that results in attraction versus feeling threatened or put off.

Perceptive leaders know how to craft messages to meet the needs of target audiences; they understand what those audiences will discard out of hand and what hot buttons will pique their interest. There is an entire behavioral discipline behind effectively communicating through the casting of positive perception, and when one masters it, one's achievements can become the stuff of legend. The key to that mastery resides in one's ability to read audiences and predict behavior, based on an inherent understanding of the audience's values and how those values become filters for everything the audience observes in the world.

The ability to master perception is only one element of what is known as social intelligence, which studies have proved—as we've covered in depth in this book—to be a separate realm of human psychology from cognitive intelligence or emotional intelligence. Although the science of social intelligence is broad, we've boiled it down to seven principles, each of which places the perception of others at the forefront of executive presence. Cynics may consider this manipulative, but the fact is that all people make choices in regard to their tone, perspective, and content with each and every form of communication they undertake, including their posture and body language; thus, a thoughtful set of choices is no more manipulative than a careless one is deliberately self-destructive. The steps we've outlined include proactive engagement and self-analysis, authenticity and simplicity, empathetic thinking and listening, and a step-by-step plan to implement those tools in one's life and career.

There still may be some fortunate DNA lurking in the mix, but more likely a charismatic leader, the one people flock toward and line up behind, is a product of a strategic approach that creates wins for everyone within earshot. One subtle aspect of that ability is an understanding of how to gain buy-in and how buy-in differs in a critical way from compliance. Compliance, as you understand by now, is the avoidance of negative consequences, such as punishment for not executing an order by a superior or for failing to obey a law. Buy-in, in contrast, is a shared vision that is based on unified values, one that defines subsequent behaviors that lead toward the achievement of a common goal. Taking one for the team, for example, is much easier to swallow in the presence of buy-in than it is in a context of compliance. Athletes don't run plays because of compliance—do this or you'll run laps—they execute their role in quest of a common goal that ends up being displayed on the scoreboard. Engineering buy-in is the key to long-term motivation and determines a leader's legacy of success within an organization.

As was discussed in this book, one method of influencing others to buy in is to employ the craft of storytelling in describing the complexities of projects, initiatives, and goals. Techniques that make this more effective include picking a universal theme (a David and Goliath metaphor, for example), giving the audience credit through brevity and understatement, transporting the listener through colorful language, and using a simple and transparent structure for the story. The audience members know you're making a point from the outset, and that creates a context that can be harnessed to enlist them on both an emotional level and an intellectual level. It's hard to imagine a compliance-reliant pitch rendered in a storytelling format, and for good reason: No one wants to hear that story.

An element of the same evolution that is moving leadership from compliance-driven to buy-in-dependent executive presence is the ability of constituencies to recognize quickly and easily and then reject attempts at manipulation. No longer will motivational tactics such as "because I'm in charge" and "you get to keep your job" fly in a progressive corporate culture, and if the culture isn't progressive yet, such approaches may be precisely the reason.

Enlightened executives and managers who earn the respect of their peers, direct reports, and bosses achieve buy-in and create motivation through an understanding of the human psychology behind behaviors, attitudes, and beliefs. Effective change must be approached on this front, and achieving it requires the employment of a set of techniques and principles that are the antithesis of old school, compliance-driven management. At its heart is a truth: Compliance serves the needs of the manipulator, whereas buy-in serves the needs of a greater good.

Of course, executive presence is not all pep rallies, compelling narrative, and motivational strategies; it also involves problem solving and having the tough conversations that constitute the ups and downs of surviving and flourishing in a corporate culture. All these enlightened principles and techniques empower success in this realm as well, since they avoid manipulation and the heavy hand of vested authority in favor of shared values and clear understanding. The approach embraces subtleties such as body language, tonality, context, using questions as a tool versus dictating, and generally bringing the other party into the discussion in a way that creates a platform for mutual understanding and subsequent action. If the context of buy-in (versus compliance) already has become cultural, disciplinary and challenging conversations by nature already are empowered to achieve greater effectiveness.

This same approach applies to crisis communication as well. A crisis creates a context of urgency that can diffuse the principles of proactively enlightened management presence, and the key to success here is preparation, as we've outlined in this book. Having a crisis playbook at hand is a critical CEO tool in today's environment, one that not only addresses the preservation of the CEO's good name but deals with issues with equal parts sensitivity, clarity, and sensibility.

Before reading this book you may have had a more narrow view of branding and what it means in the business world and for one's professional reputation. *Branding* is a word that is beginning to have universal reach and weight. To boost executive presence, branding is imperative. There are actually three realms of branding, all relevant to a progressive CEO: external (as perceived in the market), internal (as perceived and exemplified by the workforce), and personal. This book has shown you the ways and the principles that lead to the creation and promotion of a personal brand that results in a powerful executive presence. Although the tools and techniques for personal branding (online social communities and blogs, for example) are perhaps different in nature and scope from those traditionally employed to craft corporate and product brands (although, as you've learned here, online venues are emerging as a primary branding tool), the essence of the mission is the same: You are attempting to influence the perception of an audience and stand out by projecting positive qualities and bonding with your constituents in meaningful ways that help you meet your professional and personal objectives.

To help in this endeavor and amplify your developing executive poise, you now have a better understanding that working with various media no longer refers simply to broadcast and print and that online venues have emerged to alter the landscape of branding in ways an enlightened CEO is obliged to embrace. Inherent to that understanding is a respectful relationship with the media that is colored by a progressive take on digital media, since the media more and more are relying on digital resources to find angles and raw data. Layered on top of all this as you develop your executive power is the need to manage search engine exposure proactively because this is the gateway to garnering an online audience. All these skills are new or greatly altered within the last decade, and enlightened executives—including CEOs—need to know not only how to speak the language but how to walk the digital walk of branding, both for the company and for themselves.

It's definitely not your father's company anymore, and even if your father was the CEO, you need to understand the new world of empowered leadership. The presence and essence of the effective CEO have changed markedly in the last two decades, and since the techniques are available to all and the standards are now universal, there is no hiding behind a title. Executive presence is the key to moving up and, once you are there, to becoming optimally effective.

Index

About the Author

Harrison Monarth is the Founder and President of GuruMaker–School of Professional Speaking, a high-impact communications consulting firm that counts Fortune 500 executives, professionals, and political candidates among its clients. Through GuruMaker, he has assembled a select team of coaches, trainers, and behavior change experts, who work together to help clients overcome their most challenging communication issues and influence important events through the skill of public discourse. Harrison has been a sought-after authority in the field of confidential executive presentation coaching for more than a decade. He has helped executives and corporate leaders from top companies throughout Europe and the United States prepare and deliver crucial business presentations. He advises companies on their communication and media strategies and helps executives craft compelling messages to the public. He is a specialist in persuasive communication and reducing conflict and crisis through effective messaging, and is frequently called upon when the stakes are high and audiences need persuading. His first book, *The Confident Speaker*, became a *New York Times* bestseller.

Harrison has personally coached senior corporate leaders from top companies such as Merrill Lynch, Hertz, Intel, and Cisco Systems, as well as the American Heart Association and the Abraham Lincoln Presidential Library and Museum. He also provides coaching and message development services to various members of the United States' Congress.

Harrison regularly travels between Los Angeles, his home in Denver, Colorado, and Washington, D.C., and makes frequent trips to Europe for his overseas clients.